Remembering That It Happened Once

Remembering That It Happened Once

Christmas Carmen for Spiritual Life All Year Long

Edited by

Dennis L. Johnson

Foreword by
Bonnie Bowman Thurston

RESOURCE *Publications* · Eugene, Oregon

Permissions

Domina, Lynn: "Leaves" from *Christian Century*, December 6, 2017. Copyright © *Christian Century* 2017. Used with permission of the publisher. "Three Kings Pass My House on a Dusky December Afternoon." Used by permission of the author. www.lynndomina.com.

Fanthorpe, U. A.: "The Wicked Fairy at the Manger," "What the Donkey Saw," "I am Joseph," Lullaby: Sanctus Deus," "The Tree," and "Not the Millennium" from *New & Collected Poems* (Enitharmon Editions, 2010). Used by permission of the publisher and the estate of UA Fanthorpe. https://enitharmon.co.uk.

Ferlinghetti, Lawrence, "Christ Climbed Down," from *A Coney Island of the Mind*, copyright ©1958 by Lawrence Ferlinghetti. Reprinted by permission of New Direction Publishing Corp. www.ndbooks.com.

Fields, Leslie Leyland: "Let the Stable Still Astonish" and "No Country for Two Kings." Used by permission of the author. www.leslieleylandfields.com.

Gioia, Dana: "Tinsel, Frankincense, and Fir" and "For the Birth of Christ." Used by permission of the author. http://danagioia.com.

Guite, Malcolm: "Christmas on the Edge" from Sounding the Seasons by Malcolm Guite. Copyright © Malcolm Guite, 2012. Published by Canterbury Press. Used by permission.

Kamienska, Anna: "Those Who Carry" and "Lack of Faith" from *Astonishments: Selected Poems of Anna Kamienska* Edited and Translated by Grazyna Drabik and David Curzon. Polish text copyright 2017 by Pawel Spiewak. Translation and compilation copyright 2007 by Grazyna Drabik and David Curzon. Used by permission of Paraclete Press. www.paracletepress.com.

Kooser, Ted: "Christmas Mail," from *Poems* (Heron Press, 2012), "Harness Bells," and "A Ringer of Bells." Used by permission of the author. www.tedkooser.net.

Lee, Karen An-Hwei: "Healing Prayer from Revelation," "The Bird Coop in Winter." Used by permission of the author. www.karenanhweilee.com.

Lee, Li-Young, "Nativity" from *Book of My Nights*. Copyright © 2001 by Li-Young Lee. Reprinted by permission of The Permissions Company, Inc., on behalf of BOA Editions, Ltd., www.boaeditions.org.

To our daughter Megan,
who as a child recited when swinging
the R. L. Stevenson poem her grandparents taught her . . .

How do you like to go up in a swing,
Up in the air so blue?
Oh, I do think it the pleasantest thing
Ever a child can do!
Up in the air and over the wall,
Till I can see so wide,
Rivers and trees and cattle and all
Over the countryside—
Till I look down on the garden green,
Down on the roof so brown—
Up in the air I go flying again,
Up in the air and down!

Contents

Foreword by Bonnie Bowman Thurston | xix

The Preface Poem: Sabbath Poem, 1987, VI—WENDELL BERRY | 1
Introduction | 3
Prologos | 27

I. Behold, I Will Tell You a Mystery | 29

The Darkest Midnight—FROM THE KILMORE CAROLS | 31
Welcome All Wonders in One Sight!—RICHARD CRASHAW | 32
Silent Night—BONNIE BOWMAN THURSTON | 33
Of the Father's Love Begotten—PRUDENTIUS | 34
For Christmas Day—LUKE WADDINGE | 37
On the Mystery of the Incarnation—DENISE LEVERTOV | 38
Revery—FENTON JOHNSON | 39
Not the Millennium—U. A. FANTHORPE | 40
Ave Maria Gratia Plena—OSCAR WILDE | 41
Sharon's Christmas Prayer—JOHN SHEA | 42
Lucubrations—BONNIE BOWMAN THURSTON | 44
Christmas Day, 1689—SOR (SISTER) JUANA INÉS DE LA CRUZ | 45
Good is the Flesh—BRIAN WREN | 47
The Divine Image—WILLIAM BLAKE | 48

II. Behold, the Servant of the Lord | 49

How Would You Paint God?—HARRIET MONROE | 51
The Blessed Virgin compared to the Air we Breathe—
    GERARD MANLEY HOPKINS | 53
Annunciation—JOHN DONNE | 57
Annunciation—SCOTT CAIRNS | 58
The Annunciation—JOYCE KILMER | 59

Magnificat: Annunciation—NOEL ROWE | 60

Ave! Maria!—W. E. B. DU BOIS | 61

The Black Madonna—ALBERT RICE | 62

Mary's Magnificat—HELEN BARRETT MONTGOMERY | 63

Those Who Carry—ANNA KAMIENSKA | 64

The Mother Mary: I—GEORGE MACDONALD | 65

III. Behold, Let Us Be Off to Bethlehem | 67

Make Way—BRENT NEWSOM | 69

ADVENT—PAMELA CRANSTON | 71

The Nativity of Christ—LUIS DE GÓNGORA | 72

I Saw a Stable—MARY ELIZABETH COLERIDGE | 73

Let the Stable Still Astonish—LESLIE LEYLAND FIELDS | 74

The Shepherd at the Nativity—TANIA RUNYAN | 75

The Angel at the Nativity—TANIA RUNYAN | 76

Mary at the Nativity—TANIA RUNYAN | 77

Joseph at the Nativity—TANIA RUNYAN | 78

I am Joseph—U. A. FANTHORPE | 80

Joseph and Mary—ROSCOE GILMORE STOTT | 81

The Story of the Shepherd—ANONYMOUS SPANISH CAROL | 83

A Shepherd Boy Remembers—WILDA MORRIS | 85

The Shepherd Who Stayed—THEODOSIA GARRISON | 87

Lullaby: Sanctus Deus—U. A. FANTHORPE | 89

What the Donkey Saw—U. A. FANTHORPE | 90

A Christmas Prayer—GEORGE MACDONALD | 91

The Wicked Fairy at the Manger—U. A. FANTHORPE | 92

The Innkeeper's Regrets—WILDA MORRIS | 93

How the Natal Star was Born—VIOLET NESDOLY | 94

Two Carols—EVELYN UNDERHILL | 96

The Christmas Silence—MARGARET DELAND | 98

A Song of the Virgin Mother—LOPE DE VEGA | 99

In the Carpenter's Shop—SARA TEASDALE | 101

IV. Behold, Magi from the East Arrived | 103

Far Across the Desert Floor—GEORGE MACDONALD | 105

Star Silver—CARL SANDBURG | 106

Christmastide—EMILY PAULINE JOHNSON(TEKAHIONWAKE) | 107

Nativity—SCOTT CAIRNS | 108

Contents

Christmas Eve at Sea—JOHN MASEFIELD | 110

Huron Carol—JEAN DE BRÉBEUF | 112

Christmas Carol—SARA TEASDALE | 114

The Magi—WILLIAM BUTLER YEATS | 115

The Child in the Manger—SUSAN LANGSTAFF MITCHELL | 116

The Star of the Heart—SUSAN LANGSTAFF MITCHELL | 117

Nativity—JOHN DONNE | 118

A Christmas Carol—GEORGE MACDONALD | 119

The Three Kings—HENRY WADSWORTH LONGFELLOW | 120

No Country for Two Kings—LESLIE LEYLAND FIELDS | 123

A Ballad for the Wise Men—MARGARET WIDDEMER | 125

The Gift—WILLIAM CARLOS WILLIAMS | 127

When Giving Is All We Have—ALBERTO RIOS | 129

Promise—GEORGIA DOUGLAS JOHNSON | 130

V. Behold, Ye Bells; Be Joyful, All | 131

Christmas Carol—PAUL LAURENCE DUNBAR | 133

A Christmas Carol—ROBERT HERRICK | 135

Ring Out, Wild Bells—ALFRED, LORD TENNYSON | 137

Christmas—GEORGE HERBERT | 139

Christmas—TORU DUTT | 141

Noel: Christmas Eve 1913—ROBERT BRIDGES | 142

Harness Bells—TED KOOSER | 144

Music on Christmas Morning—ANNE BRONTË | 145

Christmas Morn—ANNA DE BRÉMONT | 147

Christmas Hath a Darkness—CHRISTINA ROSSETTI | 149

Minstrels—WILLIAM WORDSWORTH | 150

Carol—KENNETH GRAHAM | 151

Carol of the Birds—*BAS-QUERCY* | 152

Christmas—JOHN BETJEMAN | 153

Christmas, 1903—JOHN MASEFIELD | 155

A Ringer of Bells—TED KOOSER | 156

The Mystic's Christmas—JOHN GREENLEAF WHITTIER | 157

Sing My Song Backwards—BRIAN WREN | 159

VI. Behold, Christmas Day Is Come | 161

Winter Trees—WILLIAM CARLOS WILLIAMS | 163

A Winter Twilight—ANGELINA WELD GRIMKÉ | 164

Contents

Stopping by Woods on a Snowy Evening—ROBERT FROST | 165

Christmas Trees—ROBERT FROST | 166

Noel—ANNE PORTER | 168

The Tree—U. A. FANTHORPE | 170

little tree—E. E. Cummings | 171

Christmas Lights—MICHAEL STALCUP | 173

Star of Wonder, Star of Light—BARBARA CROOKER | 174

Tinsel, Frankincense, and Fir—DANA GIOIA | 175

The Meeting—HENRY WADSWORTH LONGFELLOW | 176

The House of Hospitalities—THOMAS HARDY | 177

Leaves—LYNN DOMINA | 178

Blue Christmas—BARBARA CROOKER | 179

Wreaths—CAROLYN HILLMAN | 180

The Christmas Wreath—ANNA DE BRÉMONT | 181

For the Birth of Christ—DANA GIOIA | 182

Lack of Faith—ANNA KAMIENSKA | 183

Into the Darkest Hour—MADELEINE L'ENGLE | 184

A Christmas Carol—SAMUEL TAYLOR COLERIDGE | 185

To Jesus On His Birthday—EDNA ST. VINCENT MILLAY | 187

Christmas Bells—HENRY WADSWORTH LONGFELLOW | 188

A Christmas Carmen—JOHN GREENLEAF WHITTIER | 190

Wartime Christmas—JOYCE KILMER | 192

A Belgian Christmas Eve—ALFRED NOYES | 193

Christmas Carols—CHRISTINA ROSSETTI | 194

Christmas—CHARLES WILLIAMS | 197

Moonless Darkness Stands Between—GERARD MANLEY HOPKINS | 199

What Will it Take?—WILDA MORRIS | 200

Christmas On the Edge—MALCOLM GUITE | 201

Christmas Is Waiting to be Born—HOWARD THURMAN | 202

VII. Christmas Day and Every Day All Year Long | 203

The Festival of the Nativity—RICHARD DE LEDREDE | 205

In Tenebris—FORD MADOX FORD | 206

How the Light Comes—JAN RICHARDSON | 207

Nativity—BARBARA CROOKER | 209

Christmas Day—BRENT NEWSOM | 211

Breathe—MICHAEL STALCUP | 213

Birth—KATE MCILHAGGA | 214

Contents

Nativity—LI-YOUNG LEE | 215

Christmas Greetings from a Fairy to a Child—LEWIS CARROLL | 216

The Bird Coop in Winter—KAREN AN-HWEI LEE | 217

Three Magi Pass My House on a Dusky December
Afternoon—LYNN DOMINA | 218

Too Wise Men—FRANK X WALKER | 220

The Meteorology of Loss—BARBARA CROOKER | 221

Christmas Mail—TED KOOSER | 223

Christ Climbed Down—LAWRENCE FERLINGHETTI | 224

Sugar Mice—CAROLYN HILLMAN | 227

The House of Christmas—G. K. CHESTERTON | 229

The Gate of Eternal Blessings—WU LI | 231

Christmas—JONATHAN CHAVES | 232

A Christmas Hymn—RICHARD WATSON GILDER | 233

Christmas in the Heart—PAUL LAURENCE DUNBAR | 234

In the Bleak Midwinter—CHRISTINA ROSSETTI | 236

The Descent of the Child—SUSAN LANGSTAFF MITCHELL | 237

Christmas Song of the Old Children—GEORGE MACDONALD | 238

And Can This Newborn Mystery—BRIAN WREN | 240

And So the Word had Breath—ALFRED, LORD TENNYSON | 241

The Work of Christmas—HOWARD THURMAN | 242

Christ Has No Body—TERESA OF AVILA | 243

Epilogos: Healing Prayer from Revelation—KAREN AN-HWEI LEE | 245

Benedictus: From Light to Light—RAMI SHAPIRO | 247

For Further Reading and Reflection | 249

Personal Appreciations | 251

The Poets | 253

Bibliography | 269

Foreword

ALMOST EVERYONE ENJOYS CHRISTMAS, even (maybe especially?) non-Christians. Certainly businesses do. They put up the lights and decorations, and put out the Christmas merchandise before Advent, even (in the U.S.A.) before Thanksgiving. I've observed that those who *never* sing the hymns in ordinary worship services lustily sing carols and Christmas hymns at Christmas Eve or Christmas Day liturgies.

It's easy to be intrigued by a virgin mother or moved by the story of "no room at the inn:" the husband struggling to care for his wife, the young wife pregnant with her first baby which she delivers in a stable (which was probably really a cave, as the Church of the Nativity in Bethlehem makes clear). All this apparently was ignored by everyone but the low-on-the-social-totem-pole shepherds . . . and the angels, of course. The romance of the story has spawned many a sappy film and hundreds of doggerel filled greeting cards with images that bear no resemblance to the grim realities of that refugee family, or what their son signaled.

With its almost ready-made images, Christmas, celebrated as it is by cultural accretions that are not even vaguely scriptural, is more jolly than incarnational. In cooing over the baby and his mother it's easy to forget what he means, who he is, why he came. Cheerful Christmas lights can obscure the shadow of the cross and even the light of resurrection. Incarnation (from the Latin *in caro*, in flesh) is the staggering meaning of what Christians celebrate at Christmas. Incarnation means giving concrete, material, or bodily form to something infinitely ephemeral. Christmas celebrates the jaw dropping assertion that God came among us, *as we are*, "Eternity shut in a span" as Richard Crashaw's poem "On the Holy Nativity of our Lord God" puts it.

This is the witness of the New Testament. Writing to the Church at Philippi Paul quotes a hymn that suggests God "emptied himself," was "born in human likeness," and was "found in human form." (Philippians

2:7) Some decades later, St. John opened his gospel with a hymn to the *logos* which explained that "the Word became flesh and lived among us." (John 1:14) The claim is that God, who theistic religions take to be "spirit" not "carnal" (Jesus, himself, said as much to a Samaritan woman, "God is spirit," John 4:24), *chooses* to become flesh and, thereby, subject to human limitation. I am a Christian and readily admit that this is an outrageous claim. But the Incarnation is the root meaning of Christmas and why we celebrate it. God came to us, became us as we are, and, eventually, took our humanity back to the divine realm at Jesus' resurrection from the dead (yet another outrageous claim).

How do we begin to explain this? Or even to make language about it? Even the most exacting or elegant prose seems too brittle a form to describe a mystery which, by definition, is inexplicable. Traditionally in religious discourse speaking the "unspeakable or un-known" is done by metaphor, by comparison of what we do know with what we can't completely explain. For example, Hebrew scripture suggests YHWH is *like* a judge, a warrior, a shepherd. It is by metaphor that we attempt to make language about the unspeakable, the mysterious, all that hovers just at the edge of human perception.

I am thinking here about poetry which at its best uses what we do know to point to what we don't or can't. Poetry allows us to glimpse what might otherwise be seen only "in a mirror dimly" or, in an older translation, "through a glass darkly," a famous metaphor coined by St. Paul. (1 Corinthians 13:12) Certainly this is true of Jesus' story, and he, himself, taught in figurative language, in parables, literally two things "thrown together" to illustrate a point or suggest a conundrum. Something about Jesus' Incarnation seemed to make people break into hymns/poetry. St. Luke suggested even the angels did so at his birth. (2:13–14) What the earliest Christians thought about Jesus is quoted by St. Paul in "Christ hymns" in Philippians 2:5–11 and Colossians 1:15–20. (And there are snippets of early hymns throughout Paul's writing.) The church first expressed Christology in hymns which are, of course, poetry. The infancy story in Luke is constructed around poetry: Mary's song (1:46–55); Zechariah's prophecy (1:68–79) and that of Simeon (2:29–32). The great theological introduction to the Incarnation, John 1:1–18, is treated by the major critical commentaries as a hymn.

"As it was in the beginning," so it is now. As this extraordinary collection demonstrates, people continue to ponder the Incarnation via the medium of poetry. Brought in chorus here are many voices, male and female, from many eras of human history, and many cultures and religious traditions. Their "songs" remind us that Incarnation is a mystery to be pondered at all times and places and in every season. Opening with one of the loveliest essays on poetry you will ever read, the collection demonstrates that, in a world illumined by Incarnation, everything mirrors God, shows us, in the words of Wendell Berry in the Preface Poem, ". . . our place/Holy, although we knew it not."

Although the book contains conventionally Christian devotional poetry, its scope goes beyond what might be narrowly defined as "Christian." I suspect this is because its editor understood that "God with" the human family has implications bigger than any single religious tradition. The book's opening "stanzas" follow roughly the narrative of "the Mystery of the Incarnation," and thereafter invite the reader "to Widen the Imagination," to "Linger and Listen," to behold and remember "the Gifts of Starlight and Strangers," to "Wake and Worship and Rejoice," to remember "Nothing Now is Common Anymore," and that "Holy Mystery Permeates All Being."

In addition to the line from a Howard Thurman poem, "CHRISTMAS IS WAITING TO BE BORN" (capitals in the original), this anthology put me in mind of Meister Eckhart's dictum that "We are all meant to be Mothers of God for God is always needing to be born." This is both the hard truth of "The uncontrollable mystery on the bestial floor" ("The Magi" by William Butler Yeats) and the lovely insight of Malcolm Guite that "The end begins, the tomb becomes a womb,/ For now in him all things are realigned." ("Christmas on the Edge") The poets included here are Christian and not, well known, lesser known, and some (to me) heretofore unknown. Happily, the book includes a biographical entry for every poet and a bibliographical reference for every poem.

A lifetime's labor of love by its editor, this book is undoubtedly one of the richest sources available in English for Advent, Christmas, and Epiphany prayer and meditation. Herein is much new material for the pastor pondering how to proclaim afresh "the old, old story of Jesus and His love." But its breadth will appeal to the "spiritual but not religious," and also provide solace for those whom Christians and the church have disappointed or abused, those who can no longer bear to open a breviary, prayer book or Bible, but who still long for the God Christmas heralds. Herein there is gentle explanation for those who don't quite "get" why Christians are annually so "on about" Christmas. It truly *is* a book of "Christmas Carmen" for all year long. These are poems for anyone, at any time, who wants to explore, or who longs for deeper understanding of the profound and glorious mystery that, as the Jesuit poet Gerard Manley Hopkins wrote, "The world is charged with the grandeur of God." For those with eyes to see and ears to hear, everything pulsates with divinity, a mystery that poetry and poets help us to experience.

Bonnie Thurston
The Anchorage, Wheeling, WV, USA

The Preface Poem

Sabbath Poem, 1987, VI

Wendell Berry

Remembering that it happened once,
We cannot turn away the thought,
As we go out, to our barns
Toward the long night's end, that we
Ourselves are living in the world
It happened in when it first happened,
That we ourselves, opening a stall
(A latch thrown open countless times
Before), might find them breathing there,
Foreknown: the Child bedded in straw,
The mother kneeling over Him,
The husband standing in belief
He scarcely can believe, in light
That lights them from no source we see,
An April morning's light, the air
Around them joyful as a choir.
We stand with one hand on the door,
Looking into another world
That is this world, the pale daylight
Coming just as before, our chores
To do, the cattle all awake,
Our own white frozen breath hanging
In front of us; and we are here
As we have never been before,
Sighted as not before, our place
Holy, although we knew it not.

Introduction

I TRACE MY ATTACHMENT to poetry back to my growing up years in our family Presbyterian church in western Illinois farm country. The way it happened was not because the preachers of my childhood and youth were fond of quoting poetry (which they were not), but because together as a congregational choir we sang poetry. Sadly, that church building is long gone. All that remains is an empty corner lot. But I still have that 1955 Presbyterian hymnbook with all the poems we sang in that place. The poems fascinated me and endeared poetry to me from then on. They nurtured my faith and shaped me. They got into my memory.

There is a lovely verse of Hebrew poetry in the closing chapter of Hosea: "Take words with you/ and return to the LORD."[1] The words I sang in worship I take with me. I carry them as cherished traveling companions on the journey. They help me remember. They return me to the Lord.

Remembering

"Much of what the Bible demands can be
comprised in one word: Remember!"[2]

—RABBI ABRAHAM JOSHUA HESCHEL

"Remembering that it happened once," begins the farmer-poet in his Sabbath poem. Remembering. Our Creator has bestowed to us the priceless gift of memory and has graced us with the astounding capability to remember.

1. Hosea 14:2 (NRSV).
2. Heschel, *Man*, 162.

At the heart of Hebrew and Christian Scriptures is this gift and grace of memory and remembering.

From front to finish, the Bible summons us, invites us, implores us to remember.

> This shall be a day of remembrance for you. You shall celebrate it as a festival to the Lord . . . Moses said to the people, "Remember this day on which you came out of Egypt, out of the house of slavery, because the Lord brought you out of there with the strength of hand . . ." In every place where I cause my name to be remembered I will come to you and bless you.[3]

> The Lord said to Moses: Speak to the Israelites, and tell them to make fringes on the corners of their garments throughout their generations . . . You have the fringe so that, when you see it, you will remember all the commandments of the Lord and do them . . . So you shall remember and do all my commandments, and you shall be holy to your God.[4]

> But take care and watch yourselves closely, so as neither to forget the things that your eyes have seen nor to let them slip from your mind all the days of your life; make them known to your children and your children's children . . . Remember the long way the Lord your God has led you these forty years in the wilderness, in order to humble you, testing you to know what was in your heart, whether or not you would keep his commandments.[5]

> Remember the days of old,
>   consider the years long past;
> ask your father, and he will inform you;
>   your elders, and they will tell you.[6]

> Glory in his holy name;
>   let the hearts of those who seek the LORD rejoice.
> Seek the LORD and his strength,
>   seek his presence continually.
> Remember the wonderful works the LORD has done,
>   his miracles, and the judgments he uttered.[7]

---

3. Exodus 12:14; 13:3; 20:24b (NRSV).

4. Numbers 15:37–40 (NRSV).

5. Deuteronomy 4:9; 8:2 (NRSV).

6. Deuteronomy 32:7 (NRSV).

7. 1 Chronicles 16:10–12 (NRSV).

As a prayerbook for the people of God, the Psalms accentuate remembering:

> All the ends of the earth shall remember
>> and turn to the LORD;
> and all the families of the nations
>> shall worship before him.[8]

> These things shall I remember
>> as I pour out my soul:
> how I went with the throng,
>> and led them in procession to the house of God,
> with glad shouts and songs of thanksgiving,
>> a multitude keeping festival . . . .
> My soul is cast down within me;
>> therefore I remember you.[9]

> I consider the days of old
>> and remember the years of long go.
> I commune with my heart in the night;
>> I meditate and search my spirit . . .
> I will call to mind the deeds of the LORD;
>> I will remember your wonders of old.
> I will meditate on all your work,
>> and muse on your mighty deeds.[10]

> They remembered that God was their rock,
>> the Most High God their redeemer.[11]

> By the rivers of Babylon—
>> there we sat down and there we wept
>> when we remembered Zion.
> Let my tongue cling to the roof of my mouth,
>> if I do not remember you.[12]

Henri Nouwen reminds us, "When Israel remembers God's great acts of love and compassion, she enters into these great acts themselves. To

8. 22:27 (NRSV).

9. 42:4, 6 (NRSV).

10. 77:5, 6, 11, 12 (NRSV).

11. 78:35 (NRSV).

12. 137:1, 6 (NRSV).

remember is not simply to look back at past events; more importantly, it is to bring these events into the present and celebrate them here and now."[13]

The New Testament calls us to remember, as well:

"Remember the word that I said to you," demands Jesus.[14]

"Remember Jesus Christ, raised from the dead, a descendant of David—that is my gospel, for which I suffer hardship," implores Paul.[15]

"Remember then what you received and heard; obey it and repent," the Spirit says to the churches in the Revelation to John.[16]

"Then Jesus took a loaf of bread, and when he had given thanks, he broke it and gave it to them, saying, 'This is my body, which is given for you. Do this in remembrance of me.'"[17]

The remembering the Bible demands is not reminiscing. As Frederick Buechner notes, "When Jesus said, 'Do this in remembrance of me,' he was not prescribing a periodic slug of nostalgia."[18] Biblical remembering is not the living present returning to the dead past. It is to harken back and muse over the dead past and summon it into the living present. It is an intentional act of the will to re-member, to re-call, to re-collect, to re-connect what happened once into this day and moment for celebration, transformation, and formation.

Biblical faith as encountering and trusting God's presence, guidance, and activity, as encountering and trusting Jesus and the Spirit, is grounded in remembering. Rejoicing is rooted in remembering. Repentance, the change of heart and mind and direction, begins with remembering. Prayer ascends from remembering. Strength for today and hope—bright hope—for tomorrow[19] arise when "this I call to mind:"

13. Nouwen, *Living Reminder*, 38.

14. John 15:20 (NRSV).

15. 2 Timothy 2:8 (NRSV).

16. Revelation 3:3 (NRSV).

17. Luke 22:19 (NRSV).

18. Buechner, *Wishful*, "Memory," 58.

19. Phrases from the hymn, "Great Is Thy Faithfulness," Thomas Chisholm, 1923.

The steadfast love of the Lord never ceases,
    his mercies never come to an end;
they are new every morning;
    great is your faithfulness.[20]

Communion with Christ in the present at The Table comes with our eating and our drinking and our remembering.

The words of Scripture by the work of the Spirit have the power to change our being and doing and to shape our souls in the image of the living Word if we remember what we are called to remember. The Latin word for "remember" is *memento*. In late Middle English, *memento* was a prayer of remembrance. Ash Wednesday solemnly confronts us with, "*Memento mori*." Remember your death; remember that you are dust and to dust you shall return. *Memento*. When I hear *memento*, I think of objects I have purchased during trips or seashells picked up on the beach or pictures arranged in albums, each serving to remind me of special people or places or moments or events that have touched and enriched my life. Each is a keepsake, a remembrance, a memento that it happened once. Scripture is a holy memento of sacred stories and hallowed actions bidding us to re-call and re-enter them, to commemorate and celebrate them.

Storyteller, theologian, and poet John Shea defines sin as, among other things, having a short memory.[21] We sin, we miss the mark, when we fail to remember as Scripture bids us to do. Spiritual amnesia is an obstacle to experiencing an enthralling God-intended, Christ-embodied, and Spirit-activated life abundant and life together. So, the Bible demands, "Remember!" *Memento*.

A Way of Remembering

"Poetry is a way of remembering what it would impoverish us to forget."

—ROBERT FROST

20. Lamentations 3:21–23 (NRSV).

21. Shea, *Experience*, 77.

In a letter to a friend, Robert Frost called his poem, "Stopping by Woods on a Snowy Evening," "my best bid for remembrance."[22] His statement is just as ambiguously intriguing as his poem. Did he mean he considered that particular poem of all his poems to be the best chance for him being remembered? He is remembered, of course, for the poem, but given what he asserts is the purpose of poetry, I hear him also saying at a deeper level that the poem may be his "best bid for remembrance," not of him, but remembrance of "what it would impoverish us to forget." What the poem shows—stopping, pausing, being still, being present to the wonder around you, reflecting along the way, and resuming the journey—would be impoverishing if forgotten and we failed to do the same. Poetry invokes remembrance of what enriches our existence.

If something new is to be created—a new depth of self and soul, a new way of being human in the world and being together, a new beginning, a new direction, a new experience of Spirit—the venture begins with remembering. To live as the beloved of God and live as God's beloved community, we must remember the past. We do not outgrow the past; we grow out of the past. To grow out of the past, we must remember truthfully, honestly, transparently. All critical, transformational conversations with God, with myself, between individuals, among neighbors, as a nation and as nations, begin with remembering rather than denying or distorting or forgetting the past. What begins with remembering is sustained by remembering, and poets help us do this, as they always have.

Poetry, remember, is the oldest form of literature. Poetry existed before there was writing, which means that before there was recorded history, there was poetry. In ancient Greece, the primary method of transmitting memory was through poetry, either recited or sung. In Greek mythology, the Muses, whose task is to preserve the memory of the mythic past, are the daughters of Memory (Mnemosyne). The Muses give poets hallowed memory, creative imagination, and poetic expression and inspiration. They are daughters of Memory in the service of memory.

As ministers of memory, poems have, in many forms over many centuries, served to console, to guide, to instruct, to confront, to woo, to delight, to explore, to transform, to enchant and enrich, to heal and make whole. Through memory and remembering, poetry opens pathways to a sense of Presence and a sensation of being alive.

22. Tuten, *Robert Frost*, 347.

Nearly one-third of the Hebrew Bible is poetry, composed as hymns, songs, proverbs, lamentations, prophetic speeches, and wisdom writings. The poetry of the Bible comes to us with rich metaphoric language shaped with irony and imagery, simile and symbol, pun and paradox, pattern and personification, rhyme and rhythm, figure-of-speech and play-on-words. The psalmists use poetry to praise and pray. The prophets use poetry to persuade and prod. The sages use poetry to shepherd and school. For centuries, the people of God have been praying with poetry, been spiritually formed by poetry, and been remembering with poetry what happened once.

In the Introduction to his *Reflection on the Psalms*, C. S. Lewis tells us:

> "The Psalms were written by many poets and at many different dates . . . The Psalms are poems, and poems are intended to be sung: not doctrinal treaties, nor even sermons. Those who talk of reading the Bible 'as literature' sometimes mean, I think, reading it without attending to the main thing it is about; like reading Burke with no interest in politics, or reading the *Aeneid* with no interest in Rome. That seems to me to be nonsense . . . Most emphatically the Psalms must be read as poems; as lyrics, with all the licences and all the formalities, the hyperboles, the emotional rather than logical connections, which are proper to lyric poetry. They must be read as poems if they are to be understood . . . Otherwise we shall miss what is in them and think we see what is not.
>
> "Our Lord, soaked in the poetic tradition of His country, delighted to use (poetic parallelism) . . . 'Ask, and it will be given to you; seek, and you shall find; knock and it shall be opened to you.' . . . (B)y giving to truths this rhythmic and incantatory expression, He made them almost impossible to forget."[23]

The poetry of the Psalms, like all biblical poetry and all poetry, is a way of remembering what it would impoverish us to forget.

With memorable imagery, Walter Brueggemann, in discussing the proclamation of Hebrew prophets as poets, says that we live in a prose-flattened world.[24] By "prose" he is referring to a world that is fixed and organized in settled formulas. Prose flattens the world to leave no risk, no possibility, no energy, no space or openness for surprise or newness. The prose world is closed, categorized, compartmentalized, pigeonholed, functional, utilitarian, measurable, manageable, and administered efficiently. The unknown is to be unraveled and neatly niched. No wonder. No

23. C. S. Lewis, *Reflection*, 2, 3, 5.

24. Brueggemann, *Finally*, Introduction.

---

transcendence. No mystery. Mystery is seen as a problem to be eradicated. "As long as you have mystery, you are healthy," contends G. K Chesterton. "When you destroy mystery, you create morbidity."[25] The fixed, functional, flat world is a wearisome and tiresome place, a dreary and drab place. A morbid place. "We become so beaten by prose," says Brueggemann, "that only poetic articulation has a chance to let us live."[26]

So, the Irish poet Yeats beseeches:

> Fairies, come take me out of this dull world,
> For I would ride with you upon the wind,
> Run on the top of the disheveled tide,
> And dance upon the mountains like a flame.[27]

We need the poet to help us live and ride upon the wind and dance like a flame upon the mountains, and God sends the poet. The poet comes with language that breaks open old worlds with new ways of being and seeing. The poet comes with a daring voice that dares us to be true and do differently. The poet comes with imaginative speech that assaults imagination and with creative language that entices creativity. The poet comes with a voice of vitality that releases the power of poetry—"shattering, evocative speech that breaks fixed conclusions and presses us always toward new, dangerous, imaginative possibilities."[28] The poet comes with a song to sing, and the song opens the heart and enlarges the vision of those who hear and heed. The poet comes to sing us beyond the realm of logic and reason to "comprehend what is the breadth and length and height and depth" of the Spirit's realm. Broadest and longest and highest and deepest of all is "to know the love of Christ that surpasses knowledge, so that you may be filled with all the fullness of God."[29] This is the world the poet opens to us.

This is the great world that embraces all the wonderful works of God. This is the reality our Creator created us to live in and live for and live fully, rather than the reality the rulers and powers of this present age have created. We are diminished into morbidity when we fail to remember the promise of divine presence and the possibility of divine fullness in human existence. The biblical mandate is remember and poetry is a way of remembering.

25. Chesterton, *Orthodoxy*, 28.

26. Brueggemann, 9.

27. Yeats, *Heart's Desire*, 15.

28. Brueggemann, 6.

29. Ephesians 3:18–20 (NRSV).

God, the Eternal Word, sends the poet who comes as a servant of the Eternal Word. The poet comes as a servant of hope and newness, a servant of memory and memento, calling us to remember the past and receive newness in the present. The poet comes as a servant calling us to call to mind what the Living Word requires of us for meaningful, purposeful human existence: "to do justice, and to love kindness,/ and to walk humbly with your God."[30] The poet comes as a servant with the power of poetry to help us remember what it would impoverish us to forget.

The Power of Poetry

"Poetry is a life-changing force.—For poems are not words, after all, but fire for the cold, ropes let down to the lost, something as necessary as bread in the pockets of the hungry."[31]

—MARY OLIVER

In that humble congregation of my youth, I experienced with the singing of hymns what acclaimed hymnist-poet Brian Wren has long advocated: Hymns are poetry and theology, along with being music. "A hymn is a poem, and a poem is a visual art form. The act of reading a hymn aloud helps to recover its poetry and its power to move us—the power of language, image, metaphor, and faith-expressions."[32] He conveys in words what I was experiencing in my soul and what I continue to experience whether singing a hymn as poetry and theology or reading a poem as a means of grace and growth. The poetry moves and forms me. The words come alive to me. The word incarnates.

Reflecting on the Psalms, C. S. Lewis also observed, "It seems to me appropriate, almost inevitable, that when that great Imagination which in the beginning, for Its own delight and for the delight of men and angels and (in their proper mode) of beasts, had invented and formed the whole world of Nature, submitted to express Itself in human speech, that speech should

30. Micah 6:8 (NRSV).

31. Oliver, *Handbook,* 122.

32. Wren, "Poet of Faith.

sometimes be poetry. For poetry is a little incarnation, giving body to what had been before invisible and inaudible."[33] The little incarnation speaks the invisible and inaudible to us and into us as incarnate beings.

We need poems to do what they have the power to do in "the sloppy fullness" of our humanity. Poet Dana Gioia notes, "People have sung or chanted poems to sow and reap, court reluctant lovers, march into battle, lull infants to sleep, and call the faithful to worship. Poetry gave humanity the words to get through life."[34] The little incarnation of poetry always has and always will help flesh and bone and blood, frail and flawed human beings get through life with more meaning and purpose, with more beauty and kindness, with more joy and compassion, with more gracious and hospitable hearts, with more fruitfulness of the Spirit.

A spiritual guide and mentor for me over the years has been Baptist pastor and theologian Walter Rauschenbusch (1861–1918), who petitioned in one of his *Prayers of the Social Awakening*, "Overcome our coldness and reserve that we may throw ajar the gates of our hearts and keep open house this day."[35] Coldness and reserve are the way things are in the unpoetic world. Poetry is a way God can throw ajar the gates of our hearts to the flow of Spirit and empower us to keep open house this day with the graces of faith, hope, and love.

The blessing after blessing of the little incarnation is "that its seeing is not our usual seeing, its hearing is not our usual hearing, its knowing is not our usual knowing, its will is not our usual will. In a poem, everything travels both inward and outward."[36] Poems have the capacity to alter our seeing, our hearing, our knowing, and our willing. With poetry, God the Spirit throws ajar the gates of our hearts to form us inwardly and outwardly and communally.

The exhilarating invitation of the Spirit is, "Do you want to live in little boxes and puny pigeonholes defined and determined by forces of domination with handy labels to keep people divided? Or do you want to live free to see more and be more? Do you want to live in the truly real world that embraces all the wonderful works of God, a world that encompasses all you can ever imagine and more? Do you want to live with mystery, or settle for morbidity?" The Spirit invites us to this vibrant world and sends poets to

33. Lewis, 5.
34. Gioia, "Enchantment."
35. Johnson, *Live in God*, 40.
36. Jane Hirshfield, *Ten Windows*, 12.

sing us into it. Poetry has Spirit-power for spiritual life which embraces the whole of life.

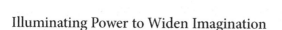

Illuminating Power to Widen Imagination

Poetry opens us to a wholly and holy different way of seeing and being in our plain, prosaic, unimaginative, uninspired world. As Jane Hirshfield observes, "The desire of monks and mystics is not unlike that of the artist: to perceive the extraordinary in the ordinary by changing not the world but the eyes that look." Poetry is how "the inner reaches out to transform the outer, and the outer reaches back to transform the one who sees."[37] A favorite poet of mine, U. A. Fanthorpe, includes in her Christmas poem "Not the Millennium" these precious lines:

> Only dull science expects
> An accurate audit. The economy of heaven
> Looks for fiestas and fireworks every day,
> Every day.
> > Be realistic, says heaven:
> Expect a miracle.

Poems "incite the imagination with unusual power,"[38] and are servants of memory helping us to live expectantly and see the miracle in the mundane of every day. Poems can move us beyond what meets the eye with an enlarged vision and expanded envisioning. Luci Shaw remembers, "It came to me, recently, that faith is 'a certain widening of the imagination.' When Mary asked the Angel, 'How shall these things be?' she was asking God to widen her imagination.

"All my life I have been requesting the same thing—a baptized imagination that has a wide enough faith to see the numinous in the ordinary. Without discarding reason, or analysis, I seek from my Muse, the Holy Spirit, images that will open up reality and pull me in to its center.

"This is the benison of the sacramental view of life."[39]

---

37. Jane Hirshfield, 12.

38. Gioia, *Enchantment*.

39. L'Engle and Shaw, *WinterSong*, 30.

Growing up in our family church, I not only found a fondness for poetry in the singing of theology, I also cut my spiritual teeth on the King James Version of the Bible. And, sure enough, come Christmas each year, I was not just accustomed to hearing but delighted in hearing over and over, "Behold!" in the birth stories of Jesus. "Behold!" is proclaimed throughout the stories, beckoning us to be grasped by glad tidings of great joy to all people. Behold, good news for an earth that is a dreary place, a troubled place, a weary place.[40] Behold! I still love that word.

Beholding is having a sanctified imagination widened with faith to see sacramentally. Beholding expects more than "dull science expects." Beholding is heavenly realistic and expects a miracle. Beholding sees more than our eyes of flesh show us. Beholding looks for fiestas and fireworks every day. Wendell Berry, going to the barn for his everyday chores "toward the long night's end," is remembering and beholding, and we are invited to do likewise.

"Remembering that it happened once," his imagination is wide enough with faith to be "Sighted as not before." Amidst the stall and straw and cattle and his "white frozen breath hanging/ In front" of him, he sees the place as Holy. He beholds the numinous in the ordinary. He finds "the Child bedded in straw," and "The mother kneeling over Him," and "The husband standing in belief/ He scarcely can believe, in light/ That lights them from no source we see." He sees sacramentally what surrounds him. He sees not just with his physical eyes, but more deeply with the eyes of his heart.

Being "Sighted as not before" is a matter of inward illumination, according to the Apostle Paul. For this reason, he prays that "the eyes of your heart may be flooded with light so that you may understand what is the hope of God's calling . . . and what is the surpassing greatness of God's might in us who believe, as seen in the energy of that resistless might which God exercised in raising Christ from the dead."[41] Poems have the power in our messy and untidy everyday humanity to transform our perception for beholding with sacramental vision, to expand our imagination for beholding beyond our imagination with the eyes of our hearts, and to be baptized with God's energy of resistless might for beholding the extraordinary in the ordinary. In union with the One C. S. Lewis names "the great Imagination," our imagination is set free and widened with faith to perceive another

40. Joyce Kilmer, "Wartime Christmas."
41. Ephesians 1:18–20. Montgomery, *New Testament.*

world not apart from this world, but within this world. This is the benison, the boon, the blessing of beholding with a sacramental view of life.

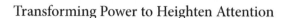

Transforming Power to Heighten Attention

With his hand on a latch he has "thrown open countless times/ Before," farmer Berry looks and becomes aware of "Looking into another world/ That is this world," and he senses being in a place as never before. His awareness is heightened with baptized imagination. He stands where he is and is blessed to behold the Holy Family and to see the place as holy. Mary Oliver says, "Sometimes, I need only stand wherever I am to be blessed."[42] Poems have the power to make us more alive to the blessedness of standing and being where we are as we have never been before.

Mary Oliver's conviction is that poetry is "a life-changing force," "fire for the cold" and "ropes let down to the lost" and bread for the hungry. With equal conviction she tells us "to pay attention, this is our endless and proper work."[43] By heightened awareness and paying attention, we come to see another world in this world. We also come to see that even our struggles with faith can throw open a latch to an experience of growth. "I have faith!" the father of a sick child cried out to Jesus. "Help my want of faith!"[44] Poet Anna Kamienska wonderfully calls that resilient, inner space of faith and growth, "A patch of wild grace."[45]

Poetry is a way of remembering to behold and pay attention to the patch of wild grace within us and in the ordinary world surrounding us. Ted Kooser, past United States Poet Laureate, has said of his poetry, "I write for other people with the hope that I can help them to see wonderful things within their everyday experiences. In short, I want to show people how interesting the ordinary world can be if you pay attention."[46] We are impoverished when we fail to pay attention, to stay awake, to be alert to every inward and outward patch of wild grace. We diminish in morbidity when

42. Oliver, *Evidence*, 21.

43. Oliver, *Handbook*, 122.

44. Mark 9:24, Goodspeed.

45. Anna Kamienska, "Lack of Faith."

46. See *Poetry Foundation*, "Ted Kooser." https://www.poetryfoundation.org/poets/ted-kooser.

we fail to be attentive in those blessed, every day, "be still and know that I am God" moments.

Look closely. Listen carefully. Linger contemplatively. Poetry directs us to wake up and worship in amazement, to look up and rejoice in enchantment, and to fall silent in gratitude and awe. Poetry frees our hearts to behold the Holy One in our midst and the holy in every day. Poetry pushes us beyond the mind and heightens our sensitivities and sensibilities for beholding into another world that is this world.

Healing Power to Deepen Communion and Connection

There is a voice speaking to us in every poem. Wendell Berry's voice in his Sabbath poem is not first-person singular; it is first-person plural. It is communal, not individual. Never "I," always "we." Never "me," always "us." Never "my," always "our." Never "myself," always "ourselves." He speaks with the voice of solidarity in the human experience of God, the Holy, the Immense, the Unknown, the Silence, the Merciful, the One Who loves, the One Who is All.[47]

Poetry has power to deepen our spiritual union with our Creator and with all creation, with Spirit and with beauty, with the sacred and with this old world God loves so much. Poetry creates communion with the poet who gives us the poem and with other poets who explore the same themes from different angles and with other images. It deepens communion with the Source of life and all life, with self and neighbor, with the living and dead, with all creation and each person we encounter. Through poetry we remember and re-member ourselves into the solidarity God has woven in the wonder of creation through Christ, the Word, "who existed before all things and who sustains and embraces all things."[48]

This power—a healing power—is released by the little incarnation of poetry. Healing is more than being physically cured. Healing is being restored to loving harmony with God, with self, with others and with creation. Out of this life-giving, holistic communion with God and all creation, our love and solidarity expand, our devotion and commitment enlarge, and our celebration and gratitude embrace the whole of the blessed and sloppy

47. Merton, *Dialogues*. xv.
48. Colossians 1:17 Goodspeed.

fullness of our common humanity. We are in communion and community as not before.

"Where life is held precious and restored and redeemed when broken or soiled," Rauschenbusch said over a century ago, "there is God's country, and the law of Christ prevails." But, he added, not "when life is held cheap and wasted needlessly, and the joy and beauty of life are turned into weariness. Death rules because love and solidarity do not rule."[49] If you have any doubt of this being true, consider the mess our country is in right now during the deadly pandemic and our bitter American racial, political and cultural divides. The truth is obviously and painfully clear. Death rules when love and solidarity do not rule. Only when broken life is held precious and redeemed and restored in love and solidarity, are we God's country. Poetry is a way of remembering the essential divine and human communion and solidarity that holds life precious and holds all life together in loving harmony. There is restoring and healing power in poetry.

Formative Power to Shape the Soul.

"One breath taken completely; one poem, fully written, fully read—in such a moment, anything can happen." [50]

—JANE HIRSHFIELD

Mark Burrows reminds us of Phillis Tickle's insight that poems have to do with educating our souls, and he suggests, "By this she meant something ancient yet utterly contemporary: the call to open ourselves to the spiritual core of our being on this earth."[51] Rauschenbusch expressed his life of prayer in his poem, "The Little Gate to God," which begins: "In the castle of my soul/ is a little garden gate,/whereat, when I enter, I am in the presence of God."[52] Poetry unlatches that little garden gate into the inner realm of our souls where we are in the presence of God. Poetry has the power to

49. Johnson, *Live in God*, 178.
50. Hirshfield, *Nine Gates*, 32.
51. Burrows, *Paraclete Anthology*, xix.
52. Johnson, *Live in God*, 18.

open our hearts and to educate our spiritual core. This soul-shaping power is released by being a reading soul. [53]

Analyzing a poem objectively, abstractly with detachment to determine what it means is, as Dana Gioia has said, "often revelatory, but seldom rapturous."[54] We do not have to be learned, expert literary critics or beneficiaries of an advanced literary education to simply enjoy a poem, to find a poem rapturous. I know from experience that the delight and pleasure, the joy and enchantment, the formative power of a poem is released when I read with openness to being formed at the core of my being on this earth.

The power of poetry to shape the soul of a soul reader gets underway, in the words of Jane Hirshfield, with "one breath taken completely." Her words are most useful as a metaphor for soul reading. Start with one breath taken completely. Not a shallow breath for shallow reading. Not a quick breath for speed reading. Not short breaths to sprint through the poem. One full breath to go deep below the surface of the poem and of myself. One complete breath with which to enter the power of slow for pausing and pondering with the poem. One complete breath that holds the mind in the soul with everything else in a matter-of-fact world that values the mind over all else. One breath fully taken for a rapturous encounter with one poem fully written. One deep breath to inhale the breath of God and be in-spired, in-fused with Holy Spirit, the Heavenly Muse.

"One breath taken completely; one poem, fully read." I take "fully read" to include reading the poem as an invitation to an experience rather than as a riddle to unknot or a puzzle to figure out or cryptic lines to decode. Poet Tania Runyan reminds us, "A poem is not a problem to be solved, but an experience to live."[55] "Fully read" includes not only reading the poem all the way through, but also permitting the poem to read me through and through. "Fully read" includes moving the poem off the page and reading it aloud. Since poetry began as an oral art long before it became a written art, poetry is meant to be heard. "Fully read" includes allowing the breath of God to breathe life into the poetic encounter. A "fully read" poem grasps and shapes a reading soul.

A reading soul approaches in a spiritual way whatever poem or literary work is being read. A reading soul follows the Spirit's promptings and is attentive to the inklings of God. As Bonnie Thurston observes, "amidst an

---

53. Runyan, *Read*, 12.

54. Gioia, *Enchantment*.

55. Runyan, *Read*, 102.

oceanic symphony,/ listen for the quiet burble/of a small stream's word."[56] With mind and heart and the mind held in the heart, we linger and listen for that quiet murmur of a small stream's word echoing the Eternal Word.

To be a reading soul reading fully is to ask, not only what does the poem mean, but what difference does that meaning make in the meaning of my life? What does the poem ask, what does it show, what does it model? What ways of being and doing, thinking and feeling, seeing and acting are displayed or endorsed or admired or confronted or conjured up?

There may be in the poem a particular word or metaphor that "cracks the mind's shell and enters the heart."[57] A reading soul lets that word or metaphor crack the mind open and slowly seep from the mind to the heart. Then, from the heart, it works its way into that reading soul's being and beholding and behaving in the world as a living reminder of Jesus, the Living Metaphor of God.

Reading fully as a reading soul is to behold Mary and do the same. She ponders all that she hears the angel tell her and she embraces it. Pause and reflect, linger and listen, contemplate and ponder all the Heavenly Muse is saying in the poetic encounter. Then embrace it.

Anything can happen with one breath taken completely. Anything can happen with the Breath of God breathing into us. Anything can happen with a poem fully read spiritually, contemplatively, deeply, prayerfully. Our imagination widens with faith. Our awareness and attentiveness heighten with sacramental vision. Our communion with the Holy One and the human community deepens with love and solidarity. The eyes of our heart are illumined, and we see as not before. The spiritual core of our being in this world is shaped by the word with our remembering. This world becomes a great world, a grand world full of all the wonderful works of God beyond comprehension and imaginings. When a soul reader's whole being is receptive to the power of poetry, doors of grace may fly open, or they may open gradually, gently, quietly. One breath taken completely; one poem, fully written, fully read. Behold, anything can happen.

So, why Christmas poems and why all year long?

---

56. Bonnie Thurston, "Lucubrations."
57. Levertov, "On the Mystery of the Incarnation."

Christmas Poems for Spiritual Life

*"When we think of Christmas, let us think of it as a
time when we remember the graces of life."*[58]

—HOWARD THURMAN

I confess, I am enamored with Christmas poetry. Not exclusively, but especially Christmas poems. Early in my ministry of over 40 years as a Baptist pastor, I was drawn to the liturgical seasons of the Christian calendar. Advent and Christmas and Epiphany captured my imagination the most. I began collecting, and continue collecting in retirement, poetry and other literary material reflecting the spirituality of Christmas, not for sermon illustrations, but for my spiritual formation in companionship with the essential Christmas stories—those "behold" stories—the birth narratives in the Gospels.

The Gospels are not biographies of Jesus akin to Sandburg's multivolume biography of Lincoln. The Gospels were composed and designed to form the faith of the spiritual communities of Matthew, Mark, Luke and John. They are intended to form us, not only to inform us. The birth narratives found in Matthew and Luke, first told as stories from memory and later written down to preserve that memory, serve the larger design of the Gospels to form our faith and shape our souls in the image of Christ for the sake of others. They are for our remembering and our formation. "Remember that it happened once," they insist, "and be re-membered into what it was that happened once."

The narratives of Jesus' birth have for centuries inspired poets to remember and retell the birth in poetic form from personal experience with cultural imagination. From the ancient past to the present day, poets have given us Christmas poems as portals to explore the stunning event and astonishing affirmation which is the bedrock of Christian faith, foundational for Christian spiritual life, and at the heart of Christmas: The Eternal Word has become human flesh in Jesus of Nazareth. "He is the visible image of the invisible God," Paul proclaims. [59] "The Grand Miracle," C. S. Lewis

---

58. Thurman, *Mood*, 12.

59. Colossians 1:15, Montgomery.

asserts. [60] "The Glorious Impossible," Madeleine L'Engle declares. [61] "And so the Word had breath," Tennyson confesses.[62] "Eternity shut in a span,"[63] Richard Crashaw heralds. This is the Christmas miracle and mystery.

"Ultimate Mystery born with a skull you could crush one-handed," Buechner says, whispering in awe, I imagine. "It is unthinkable darkness riven with unbearable light. Agonizing labor led to it, vast upheavals of intergalactic space, time split apart, a wrenching and tearing of the very sinews of reality itself. You can only cover your eyes and shudder before it . . ." Ultimate Mystery, unbearable Light, in the words of creed and carols, "came down from heaven." Came down. "Only then do we dare uncover our eyes and see what we can see."[64] The Incarnation. *O Magnum Mysterium!*

In "Star Silver," poet Carl Sandburg wonders:

> The vagabond Mother of Christ
> And the vagabond men of wisdom,
> All in a barn on a winter night,
> And a baby there in swaddling clothes on hay—
> Why does this story never wear out?"[65]

It does not wear out because, as poet John Betjeman declares, the story is the "most tremendous tale of all."[66] And the Incarnation is the most tremendous tale of all because, as poet Madeleine L'Engle insists, we Christians are

> those strange creatures who proclaim to believe that the Power that created the entire universe willingly and lovingly abdicated that power and became a human baby. Particle physics teaches us that energy and matter are interchangeable. So, for love of us recalcitrant human creatures, the sheer energy of Christ changed into the matter of Jesus, ordinary human matter, faulted, flawed, born with the seed of death already within the flesh as a sign of solidarity with our mortality. [67]

A tremendous tale that never wears out. A thought we cannot turn away.

---

60. Lewis, *Grand*, 61, 62.

61. L'Engle, *Glorious.*

62. Alfred, Lord Tennyson, "And So the Word had Breath."

63. Richard Crashaw, "Welcome All Wonders in One Sight."

64. Buechner, *Whistling*, 29.

65. Sandburg, "Star Silver."

66. Betjeman, "Christmas."

67. L'Engle, *WinterSong*, 74.

Remembering that it happened once,
We cannot turn away the thought,
As we go out, to our barns
Toward the long night's end, that we
Ourselves are living in the world
It happened in when it first happened,
That we ourselves, opening a stall
. . . might find them breathing there,
. . . in light
That lights them from no source we see,
An April morning's light, the air
Around them joyful as a choir.

All poetry, I suppose, reflects some "it" that happened once. The "it" farmer Berry on his way to the barn is remembering happened once is, of course, as Sandburg puts it, the birth of "a baby slung in a feed-box/ Back in a barn in a Bethlehem slum."[68] "Them" we find there, of course, are the Child, the mother, the husband, and all the characters and creatures at the feed-box in a barn long ago. "Who can bring back the magic of that story?" asks poet Susan Langstaff Mitchell.[69] Poets can. Poets do.

Thankfully, poetry—Christmas poetry—is a way of remembering that it happened once and "we/Ourselves are living in the world/ It happened in when it first happened."

Remembering that it happened once, poets in this collection recall "it" as, "the supreme mystery of love," the birth of a "child of fire," "the all-embracing birth" which "lifts earth to heaven, stoops heaven to earth."[70]

"It" is the silent night when "that tiny spark,/ the Word, dropped/ into kindling flesh,/ set afire everything/ we thought we knew/ about God.[71]

"It" is when "The world was lorn/ But Christ is born/ To change our sadness into glory."[72]

"It" is when, "The safety of the world was lying there,/ And the world's danger."[73]

---

68. Sandburg, "Star Silver."

69. Susan Langstaff Mitchell, "The Descent of the Child."

70. Oscar Wilde, "Ave Maria Gratia Plena;" Dana Gioia, "For the Birth of Christ;" Richard Crashaw, "Welcome All Wonders in One Sight."

71. Bonnie Thurston, "Silent Night."

72. Paul Laurence Dunbar, "Christmas Carol."

73. Mary Elizabeth Coleridge, "I Saw a Stable."

"It" is, "newborn Jesus,/ Loving great and small,/ Love's free Sacrifice,/ Opening Arms and Eyes/ To one and all."[74]

And "It calls us, with an angel's voice,/ To wake, and worship, and rejoice."[75]

This marvel of "Eternity shut in a span," this astounding change of the energy of Christ into the matter of Jesus, "also promises us that our human, mortal matter is permeated with Christ's total energy, the creative energy which shouted into being all the galaxies, hydrogen clouds, solar systems, planets, all life—even us! When Christ was born as Jesus . . . that incredible birth honored all our births, and assured us that we, God's beloved children, partake of eternal life. For indeed it follows that as Christ partook of human life, we partake of divine life."[76] *O Magnum Mysterium,* indeed. O Great Mystery. The most tremendous tale of all. The wondrous story that never wears out. Truly, a thought we cannot turn away without impoverishing ourselves in a prose-flattened world.

Nineteenth century Scottish author, poet, pastor, theologian, George MacDonald, spun the spiritual truth and beauty of Christmas with regular frequency into his stories and nonfiction and poetry. It may be a bit surprising to discover that he was virtually silent about all other church seasons and sacred days. Easter gets a lonely single mention by MacDonald in all his voluminous writing. Christmas was the "holyday" that inspired him

MacDonald writes of Christmas in a letter from 1888, "If the story were not true nothing else would be worth being true. Because it is true, everything is lovely—precious." In *Adela Cathcart,* he writes that Christmas is the day that "makes all days of the year as sacred as itself."[77]

In his 1855 poetic drama, *Within and Without,* the central character, Julian, says in an extended reflection on Christmas Day:

> the light comes feebly, slowly, to the world
> On this one day that blesses all the year . . .
> where nothing now is common anymore . . .
> Now, now we feel the holy mystery
> That permeates all being: all is God's
> And my poor life is terribly sublime.[78]

---

74. Christina Rossetti, "Christmas Carols, 3."

75. Anne Brontë, "Music on Christmas Morning."

76. L'Engle, *WinterSong,* 74

77. MacDonald, *Adela Cathcart,* 221.

78. MacDonald, *Within and Without,* 125ff.

Christmas is the "day that blesses all the year" and "nothing now is common anymore." All days of the year are made sacred by Christmas Day. Emmanuel, God with us. "The Word became flesh and tented with us."[79] The Timeless inhabits the temporal; Eternity indwells history. "The lowly and despised is shot through with glory," Rauschenbusch rejoices.[80] By remembering that it happened once, we remember all time is blessed by that time and every day is as sacred as that day when first it happened. All is God's, and your life, my life, each and every life is terribly sublime. Nothing is common anymore; therefore, all life and all things are worthy of our attention and awareness. All ground is holy ground because, as Buechner puts it, "God not only made it but walked on it, ate and slept and worked and died on it."[81] The world we live in and the earth we walk and work and eat and die on is "the world/ It happened in when it first happened." This is the holy mystery at the heart of Christmas and all existence. Howard Thurman reminds us, "The true meaning of Christmas is expressed in the sharing of one's graces in a world in which it is easy to become callous, insensitive, and hard. Once this spirit becomes part of one's life, every day is Christmas, and every night is freighted with anticipation of the dawning of fresh, and perhaps, holy, adventure."[82]

So, if you wonder, "Why Christmas poems and why all year long?", now you have my answer. Now you know why.

Dana Gioia, who writes from a Catholic, sacramental spiritual tradition and perspective, acknowledges, "I don't write for poets or literary critics. I don't write for readers of any particular faith, politics, or aesthetics. It seems a grave danger to write only for readers who share your own ideology—a kind of psychic laziness." He adds, "A religious poem, for instance, should speak to an atheist as much as a believer. It might speak differently perhaps, but it needs to transcend any system of belief and touch some common humanity. Maybe 'transcend' is the wrong word. 'Exceed' might be better . . . A poet should entice rather than exclude."[83]

The Christmas poems in this collection, I believe, entice rather than exclude. They come from different times and eras, places and people, cultures and traditions. They come from Protestants and Catholics and Orthodox and agnostics and poets inclusive of faith beyond a single tradition. They are from

---

79. John 1:14, Montgomery *New Testament.*

80. Johnson, *Live in God,* 18.

81. Buechner, *Wishful,* 43.

82. Thurman, *Deep,* 140.

83. Koss, "Conversation."

poets ancient and contemporary who, in their own time and way, experienced joy and sorrow, faith and doubt, fullness and emptiness, gratitude and grief, day light and dark night. They poetically speak their awe and despair, their questions and aspirations, their praise and disappointment, their best intentions and deepest fears and highest hopes. Some echo Christmas exultation and celebration, others lament Christmas loss and loneliness. Some, in the spirit of Christmas jubilation, "sing a glad welcoming/ To herald the Child-Christ born."[84] For others "in the houses of mourning/ the holidays weigh like a heavy sack. In the corner, the empty chair."[85] Some poems are joyful; others painful. Some evoke adoration; others express anguish. Some affirm wonder and mystery; others reveal wounds and melancholy. Some soothe the heart and spirit; others trouble the spirit and strike dissonance in the heart by confronting our hypocrisy and materialism and greed, our fear of otherness or strangers or change or the unknown or the unexpected. Some explore Incarnation in everyday life; others focus on issues of social justice as imperatives of Incarnation. Some poems from the past declare, "Peace on earth," as present in their time which might be dismissed as naïve sentimentalism and poppycock. Or it may be heard as a summons to pray for peace, work for peace, and live for peace in our time. Some poems are about Christmas; others are set during Christmas; still others simply reflect the message and mood, the spirit and spirituality of Christmas without mentioning Christmas. Some name God and Jesus. Some use theological language. Some are explicitly religious. Others do not and are not. As I read them and reflect on them, as I linger with them and listen to them, they each are tethered to Christmas intentionally or implicitly. Rather than exclude, they entice us to behold and be held by the Grand Miracle all year long.

Poems come from soul work and are given for soul work in soul readers. The poems in this collection carry the promise of opening your heart as they have opened mine. The Irish poet Seamus Heaney maintains, "If poetry and the arts do anything, they can fortify your inner life, your inwardness."[86] Every good poem speaks to that inner life and inward being where God abides. If you approach these poems as a soul reader, they may unlock your heart; they may alter your perception; they may enlarge your vision; they may enchant you into being a beholder. Each one in some way says, "Come with me in your mind's eye and the eyes of your heart and I

84. Anna de Brémont, "Christmas Morn."
85. Barbara Crooker, "Blue Christmas."
86. Lamb, "Seamus Heaney,"

will take you on a road into the most tremendous tale of all. I can help you remember that it happened once. I can help you remember that we are living in the world it happened in when it first happened." Will we let them lead us there? Will we let them help our remembering?

John Shea reminds us with his Christmas poems[87] that each figure we find in the birth narratives and place in our crèches every year, along with the animals and creatures at the Nativity we have been given by tradition and imagination, has something to tell us, to show us. In some form or fashion, they all say and show something to us about the graces of life and about an all-inclusive Love at the center of life. But will we linger with them? Will we listen to them? Will we let them open our hearts?

We are all meant to be adoring shepherds, angelic messengers, star-following Magi. We are meant to find a Joseph in ourselves, and a Herod. We are all meant to be a Mary and give birth to Christ in the time of our life in this world. We are all meant to be "New Nazareths" as a place for Christ-conception, and "New Bethlems" as a birthing place for Jesus.[88] Remember, Howard Thurman insists, "Christmas is yesterday, today, and tomorrow," and Christmas is waiting to be born in you, in me, in all humankind.[89]

The Latin word for "poetry" is *carmen*. In a roundabout way, *carmen* became our English word, "charm." Still today the word carries the meaning of a magic spell, a spoken poem,[90] and the power to enthrall.[91] My hope is these poems charm you into beholding and abiding in the mystery and wonder of the Incarnation every day for the rest of your days on this earth. My prayer is that they will enthrall you into remembering all the graces of life and beguile you into becoming empty enough to be full of grace. My heartfelt desire is that they will enchant you into opening your heart. May they captivate you into allowing your imagination to widen and your soul to be shaped. May they be Christmas carmen that entice you into birthing Christ in the flesh of you for the sake of others until

> we all become
> the kindled kindred of a King whose birth
> thereafter bears to all a bright nativity.[92]

87. Shea, *Haloes*."
88. Gerard Manley Hopkins, "The Blessed Virgin compared with the Air we Breathe."
89. Thurman, *Mood*, 21.
90. As with John Greenleaf Whittier's poem, "A Christmas Carmen."
91. Gioia, "Enchantment."
92. Scott Cairns, "Nativity."

Prologos

In the beginning the Word existed.
The Word was with God,
   and the Word was divine.
It was he that was with God in the beginning.
Everything came into existence through him,
   and apart from him
   nothing came to be.
It was by him that life came into existence,
   and that life was the light of all people.
The light is still shining in the darkness,
   for the darkness has never put it out.

From the Gospel of John, chapter 1[1]

Whilst all things were in quiet silence
   and night was in the midst of her swift course:
Thine Almighty Word leapt down from heaven
   out of thy royal throne.
      Alleluia!

Ancient Christmas Prayer

---

1. Goodspeed, *New Testament.*

"As the Christmas Day Gospel takes us back to the Mystery of the Divine Nature—*In the beginning was the Word*—so let us begin by thinking of what Catherine of Siena called the 'ocean Pacific of the Godhead' enveloping all life."

Evelyn Underhill
The Light of Christ

I

Behold, I Will Tell You a Mystery
*Poems for Beholding and Remembering
the Wonder of the Incarnation*

So the Word became flesh and blood
    and lived for a while among us,
        abounding in blessing and truth,
            and we saw the honor God had given him . . .
For from his abundance
    we have all had a share,
        and received blessing after blessing.

From the Gospel of John, chapter 1[1]

Truly there is nothing so great and wonderful as this,
    that you, my God, who are the creator of all things,
    should become a creature,
    so that we should become like God.
You have humbled yourself and made yourself small
    that we might be made mighty.
You have taken the form of a servant,
    so that you might confer upon us a royal and divine beauty.

1. Goodspeed translation

You, who are beyond understanding,
    have made yourself understandable to us in Jesus Christ.
You, who are the uncreated God,
    have made yourself a creature for us.
You, who are the untouchable One,
    have made yourself touchable to us.
You, who are most high,
    make us able to understand your amazing love.
Make us able to understand the profound mystery of your holy incarnation.

Angela of Foligno
Medieval churchwoman

The Darkest Midnight

from THE KILMORE CAROLS

The darkest midnight in December
No snow, nor hail, nor winter storm
Shall hinder us for to remember,
The Babe that on this night was born.
With shepherds we are come to see,
This lovely Infant's glorious charms,
Born of a Maid as the prophet said,
The God of love in Mary's arms.

No earthly gifts can we present Him,
No gold nor myrrh nor odors sweet.
But if with hearts we can content Him
We humbly lay them at His feet.
'Twas but pure love that from above
Brought Him to save us from all harms.
So let us sing and welcome Him,
The God of Love in Mary's arms.

Ye blessed angels join our voices
Let your gilded wings beat fluttering o'er,
While every soul set free rejoices,
And everyone now must adore.
We'll sing and pray that He always may
Good people one and all defend,
God grant us grace in all our days
A merry Christmas and a happy end.

Welcome All Wonders in One Sight!

Richard Crashaw

(a portion of "In the Holy Nativity of Our Lord God")

Gloomy night embraced the place
    Where the Noble Infant lay;
The Babe looked up and showed his face;
    In spite of darkness it was day.
It was thy day, Sweet! and did rise
Not from the east, but from thine eyes.

Winter chid aloud, and sent
    The angry North to wage his wars;
The North forgot his fierce intent,
    And left perfumes instead of scars.
By those sweet eyes' persuasive powers,
Where he meant frost, he scattered flowers.

Poor World, said I, what wilt thou do
    To entertain this starry stranger?
Is this the best thou canst bestow,
    A cold, and not too cleanly, manger?
Contend, ye powers of heaven and earth,
To fit a bed for this huge birth.

Welcome, all wonders in one sight!
    Eternity shut in a span;
Summer in winter, day in night;
    Heaven in earth, and God in man.
Great little one! whose all-embracing birth
Lifts earth to heaven, stoops heaven to earth.

Silent Night

BONNIE BOWMAN THURSTON

The old tradition says
at Christ's borning
there was utter silence.
The whole created world
was still. For an hour.
Even choirs of angels
went quiet.
It seems fitting
in the infant face
of incomprehensibility
to forego language,
sound, even song.
Into *stille nacht*
that tiny spark,
the Word, dropped
into kindling flesh,
set afire everything
we thought we knew
about God.

Of the Father's Love Begotten

Prudentius

Of the Father's love begotten,
Ere the worlds began to be,
He is Alpha and Omega,
He the source, the ending He,
Of the things that are, that have been,
And that future years shall see,
Evermore and evermore!

By His Word was all created;
He commanded and 'twas done;
Earth and sky and boundless ocean,
Universe of three in one,
All that sees the moon's soft radiance,
All that breathes beneath the sun,
Evermore and evermore!

He is found in human fashion,
Death and sorrow here to know,
That the race of Adam's children
Doomed by law to endless woe,
May not henceforth die and perish
In the dreadful gulf below,
Evermore and evermore!

O that birth forever blessed,
When the virgin, full of grace,
By the Holy Ghost conceiving,
Bore the Saviour of our race;

And the Babe, the world's Redeemer,
First revealed His sacred face,
Evermore and evermore!

O ye heights of heaven adore Him;
Angel hosts, His praises sing;
Powers, dominions, bow before Him,
And extol our God and King!
Let no tongue on earth be silent,
Every voice in concert sing,
Evermore and evermore!

This is He Whom seers in old time
Chanted of with one accord;
Whom the voices of the prophets
Promised in their faithful word;
Now He shines, the long expected,
Let creation praise its Lord,
Evermore and evermore!

Hail! Thou Judge of souls departed;
Hail! of all the living King!
On the Father's right hand throned,
Through His courts thy praises ring,
Till at last for all offenses
Righteous judgement thou shalt bring,
Evermore and evermore!

Now let old and young uniting
Chant to Thee harmonious lays,
Maid and matron hymn Thy glory,
Infant lips their anthem raise,
Boys and girls together singing
With pure heart their song of praise,
Evermore and evermore!

Let the storm and summer sunshine,
Gliding stream and sounding shore,
Sea and forest, frost and zephyr,

Day and night their Lord adore;
Let creation join to laud Thee
Through the ages evermore,
Evermore and evermore!

Christ, to Thee with God, the Father,
And, O Holy Ghost, to Thee,
Hymn and chant with high thanksgiving,
And unwearied praises be:
Honour, glory, and dominion,
And eternal victory,
Evermore and evermore!

For Christmas Day

LUKE WADDINGE

This Christmas Day you pray me sing,
My carol to our new-born King,
A God made Man, the Virgin's Son,
The Word made Flesh, can this be done?
    Of me I pray no more require
    Then this great Mystery to admire.

Whom Heaven of Heavens cannot contain,
As Scripture doth declare most plain,
In a poor stable is born this day
Lay'd in a manger wrapt in hay.
    Of me I pray no more require
    Then this great Mystery to admire.

Heaven's great treasures are now but small!
Immensity no extent at all,
Eternity's but one day old
Tho' Almighty feeleth the Winter cold,
    Of me I pray no more require
    Then this great Mystery to admire.

On the Mystery of the Incarnation

Denise Levertov

It's when we face for a moment
the worst our kind can do, and shudder to know
the taint in our own selves, that awe
cracks the mind's shell and enters the heart:
not to a flower, not to a dolphin,
to no innocent form
but to this creature vainly sure
it and no other is god-like, God
(out of compassion for our ugly
failure to evolve) entrusts,
as guest, as brother,
the Word.

Revery

FENTON JOHNSON

1.

I was the starlight
I was the moonlight
I was the sunset,
Before the dawning
    Of my life;
I was the river
Forever winding
To purple dreaming,
I was the glowing
Of youthful Springtime,
I was the singing
Of golden songbirds,—
    I was love.

2.

I was the sunlight,
I was the twilight,
I was the humming
Of winged creatures
    Ere my birth;
I was the blushing
Of lily maiden,
I was the vision
Of youthful striving,
I was the summer,
I was the autumn,
I was the All-time—
    I was love.

Not the Millennium

U. A. FANTHORPE

Wise men are busy being computer-literate.

There should be a law against confusing
Religion with mathematics.
There was a baby. Born where?
And when? The sources mention
Massacres, prophecies, stars;
They tell a good story, but they don't agree.

So we celebrate at the wrong midnight.
Does it matter? Only dull science expects
An accurate audit. The economy of heaven
Looks for fiestas and fireworks every day,
Every day.
   Be realistic, says heaven:
Expect a miracle.

Ave Maria Gratia Plena

OSCAR WILDE

Was this His coming! I had hoped to see
A scene of wondrous glory, as was told
Of some great God who in a rain of gold
Broke open bars and fell on Danaë:
Or a dread vision as when Semele,
Sickening for love and unappeased desire,
Prayed to see God's clear body, and the fire
Caught her brown limbs and slew her utterly.
With such glad dreams I sought this holy place,
And now with wondering eyes and heart I stand
Before this supreme mystery of Love:
Some kneeling girl with passionless pale face,
An angel with a lily in his hand,
And over both the white wings of a Dove.

Sharon's Christmas Prayer

JOHN SHEA

She was five,
sure of the facts,
and recited them
with slow solemnity
convinced every word
was revelation. She said:

> "They were so poor
> they had only peanut butter and jelly sandwiches
> to eat
> and they went a long way from home
> without getting lost.
> The lady rode a donkey,
> the man walked,
> and the baby was inside the lady.
> They had to stay in a stable
> with an ox and an ass (hee-hee)
> but the Three Rich Men found them
> because a star lighted the roof.
> Shepherds came and you could
> pet the sheep but not feed them.
> Then the baby was borned.
> And do you know who he was?"

Her quarter eyes inflated to silver dollars,

> "The baby was God."

And she jumped in the air,
whirled round, dove into the sofa,
and buried her head under the cushion
which is the only proper response
to the Good News of the Incarnation.

Lucubrations

BONNIE BOWMAN THURSTON

Our Lady of the Angels Monastery
Crozet, Virginia

Nestled at the base of the Blue Ridge
they begin the day at night,
as earth takes on its contours
pray their way from darkness to light,
allow another self to emerge,
the one healed of its own evil.

They wait in stillness before mystery.
Theirs is the pregnant quietude,
the darkly brilliant expectancy
of Christmas night
when the numinous depths
will deliver a virgin mother.

Their life is useless to everyone but God.
It demonstrates subtraction
is a process of freedom:
the less we own, the more we have.
It encourages increasing receptivity:
the less we grasp, the closer God comes.

Like children by a mountain brook,
they play at the edges of articulation,
amidst an oceanic symphony,
listen for the quiet burble
of a small stream's word,
and, sometimes, hear it.

Christmas Day, 1689

Sor (Sister) Juana Inés de la Cruz

Carol sung in the Cathedral of Puebla de los Angeles, in the solemn Matin of the Birth Day of our Lord Jesus Christ, this year of 1689.

Introduction

To celebrate the Child's
timely Birth,
the four elements arrive:
Water, Earth, and Air and Fire.

With good reason, since is made
the humanity of his Body
of Water, Fire, Earth and Air,
clean, pure, fragile, fresh.

In the Child the elements improve
their qualities and inner beings,
since they are given better berth
in Eyes, Breast, Flesh, Breath.

To such great favors rendered,
in loving giftgivings
they search, serve, love, adore,
promptly, delicately, purely, tenderly.

Refrain:
    And all joined together
    go to my Lord,
    that Humanized is served
    by the four elements:

Water serves his Eyes,
Air, his Breath,
Earth, his Soles,
Fire, his Breast;
that from them all, by the Child
a Whole today is made.

Good is the Flesh

BRIAN WREN

Good is the flesh that the Word has become,
    good is the birthing, the milk in the breast,
    good is the feeding, caressing and rest,
    good is the body for knowing the world,
Good is the flesh that the Word has become.

Good is the body for knowing the world,
    sensing the sunlight, the tug of the ground,
    feeling, perceiving, within and around,
    good is the body, from cradle to grave,
Good is the flesh that the Word has become.

Good is the body, from cradle to grave,
    growing and aging, arousing, impaired,
    happy in clothing, or lovingly bared,
    good is the pleasure of God in our flesh,
Good is the flesh that the Word has become.

Good is the pleasure of God in our flesh,
    longing in all, as in Jesus, to dwell,
    glad of embracing, and tasting, and smell,
    good is the body, for good and for God,
Good is the flesh that the Word has become.

The Divine Image

WILLIAM BLAKE

To Mercy, Pity, Peace, and Love
All pray in their distress;
And to these virtues of delight
Return their thankfulness.

For Mercy, Pity, Peace, and Love
Is God, our father dear,
And Mercy, Pity, Peace, and Love
Is Man, his child and care.

For Mercy has a human heart,
Pity a human face,
And Love, the human form divine,
And Peace, the human dress.

Then every man, of every clime,
That prays in his distress,
Prays to the human form divine,
Love, Mercy, Pity, Peace.

And all must love the human form,
In heathen, Turk, or Jew;
Where Mercy, Love, and Pity dwell
There God is dwelling too.

II

Behold, the Servant of the Lord

Poems for Beholding and Remembering
with Widened Imagination

The angel Gabriel was sent by God
to a town in Galilee called Nazareth,
to a virgin
engaged to a man
whose name was Joseph.
The virgin's name was Mary.
Gabriel came to her and said,
    Greetings, favored one!
    The Lord is with you.
    Do not be afraid.
    And now,
        you will conceive in your womb
        and bear a son,
        and you will name him Jesus.
    He will be great.
    He will be called Son of the Most High.
    Of his kingdom there will be no end.
Mary said to the angel,
    How can this be,
        since I am a virgin?
Gabriel said to Mary,
    The Holy Spirit will come upon you.
    The power of the Most High will overshadow you.

For nothing will be impossible with God.
Then Mary said,
>*Here am I,*
>*the servant of the Lord;*
>*let it be with me according to your word.*
Then the angel departed from her.

From the Gospel According to Luke chapter 1[1]

Almighty God,
>Grant that we who are bathed in the new light of your Incarnation
>may reflect the faith that shines in our hearts in all we do.

Tenth century Gregorian Christmas prayer

---

1. New Revised Standard Version

How Would You Paint God?

HARRIET MONROE

How would you paint God?
God, eternally young, young as the sun, young as Orion's nebula.
God the Creator, stringing worlds like pearls in the sky.
God, molding our little earth after supper of the day he
    had spread the Milky Way like a carpet for his feet;
Fingering forth men in millions with his right hand, and
    beasts, birds, fishes with his left.
God, smiling at life as at a field of nodding flowers,
Finding its good and evil good.
God fecund, magnificent, glorious.
God of the love intolerable, love dark and bright, that
    searches, challenges, rewards.
God, moving forever at the centre, with space like a thin
    robe around him.
God, facing his universe ever beginning and ending, and
    calling it a day.
God of the blazing eyes that see.
God of the secret ears that hear.
"God of God, Light of Light, very God of very God."

How would you paint God?

—Fra Angelico's Annunciation
Little virgin girl, to you the angel is bowing—
Great Gabriel, with gold-enameled wings.
Little girl in blue, dewy like a gentian at sunrise,
To you comes the angel straight from God.
So sweet, so fresh and fair—no wonder!

As clear as a spring under green leaves,
As innocent as a fluffy baby dove two or three days from
    the egg,
As still as deep-sea water—
To you the angel.

Blessed art thou amongst women, little virgin girl.

The Blessed Virgin compared to the Air we Breathe

GERARD MANLEY HOPKINS

Wild air, world-mothering air,
Nestling me everywhere,
That each eyelash or hair
Girdles; goes home betwixt
The fleeciest, frailest-flixed
Snowflake; that's fairly mixed
With, riddles, and is rife
In every least thing's life;
This needful, never spent,
And nursing element;
My more than meat and drink,
My meal at every wink;
This air, which, by life's law,
My lung must draw and draw
Now but to breathe its praise,
Minds me in many ways
Of her who not only
Gave God's infinity
Dwindled to infancy
Welcome in womb and breast,
Birth, milk, and all the rest
But mothers each new grace
That does now reach our race—
Mary Immaculate,
Merely a woman, yet
Whose presence, power is

Great as no goddess's
Was deemèd, dreamèd; who
This one work has to do—
Let all God's glory through,
God's glory which would go
Through her and from her flow
Off, and no way but so.

      I say that we are wound
With mercy round and round
As if with air: the same
Is Mary, more by name.
She, wild web, wondrous robe,
Mantels the guilty globe,
Since God has let dispense
Her prayers his providence:
Nay, more than almoner,
The sweet alms' self is her
And men are meant to share
Her life as life does air.

      If I have understood,
She holds high motherhood
Towards all our ghostly good
And plays in grace her part
About man's beating heart,
Laying, like air's fine flood,
The deathdance in his blood;
Yet no part but what will
Be Christ our Saviour still.
Of her flesh he took flesh:
He does take fresh and fresh,
Though much the mystery how,
Not flesh but spirit now
And make, O marvelous!
New Nazareths in us,
Where she shall yet conceive
Him, morning, noon, and eve;
New Bethlems, and he born
There, evening, noon, and morn

54

Bethlem or Nazareth,
Men here may draw like breath
More Christ and baffle death;
Who, born so, comes to be
New self and nobler me
In each one and each one
More makes, when all is done,
Both God's and Mary's Son.
        Again, look overhead
How air is azurèd;
O how! nay do but stand
Where you can lift your hand
Skywards: rich, rich it laps
Round the four fingergaps.
Yet such a sapphire-shot,
Charged, steepèd sky will not
Stain light. Yea, mark you this:
It does no prejudice.
The glass-blue days are those
When every colour glows,
Each shape and shadow shows.
Blue be it: this blue heaven
The seven or seven times seven
Hued sunbeam will transmit
Perfect, not alter it.
Or if there does some soft,
On things aloof, aloft,
Bloom breathe, that one breath more
Earth is the fairer for.
Whereas did air not make
This bath of blue and slake
His fire, the sun would shake,
A blear and blinding ball
With blackness bound, and all
The thick stars round him roll
Flashing like flecks of coal,
Quartz-fret, or sparks of salt,
In grimy vasty vault.

So God was god of old:
A mother came to mould
Those limbs like ours which are
What must make our daystar
Much dearer to mankind;
Whose glory bare would blind
Or less would win man's mind.
Through her we may see him
Made sweeter, not made dim,
And her hand leaves his light
Sifted to suit our sight.
    Be thou then, thou dear
Mother, my atmosphere;
To wend and meet no sin;
Above me, round me lie
Fronting my froward eye
With sweet and scarless sky;
Stir in my ears, speak there
Of God's love, O live air,
Of patience, penance, prayer:
World-mothering air, air wild,
Wound with thee, in thee isled,
Fold home, fast fold thy child.

Annunciation

John Donne

Salvation to all that will is nigh;
That All, which always is all everywhere,
Which cannot sin, and yet all sins must bear,
Which cannot die, yet cannot choose but die,
Lo, faithful virgin, yields Himself to lie
In prison, in thy womb; and though He there
Can take no sin, nor thou give, yet He will wear,
Taken from thence, flesh, which death's force may try.
Ere by the spheres time was created, thou
Wast in His mind, who is thy Son and Brother;
Whom thou conceivst, conceived; yea thou art now
Thy Maker's maker, and thy Father's mother;
Thou hast light in dark, and shutst in little room,
Immensity cloistered in thy dear womb.

Annunciation

Scott Cairns

Deep within the clay, and O my people
very deep within the wholly earthen
compound of our kind arrives of one clear,
star-illumined evening a spark igniting
once again the tinder of our lately
banked noetic fire. She burns but she
is not consumed. The dew lights gently,
suffusing the pure fleece. The wall comes down.
And—*do you feel the pulse?*—we all become
the kindled kindred of a King whose birth
thereafter bears to all a bright nativity.

The Annunciation

Joyce Kilmer

(For Helen Parry Eden)

"Hail Mary, full of grace," the Angel saith.
Our Lady bows her head, and is ashamed;
She has a Bridegroom Who may not be named,
Her mortal flesh bears Him Who conquers death.
Now in the dust her spirit grovelleth;
Too bright a Sun before her eyes has flamed,
Too fair a herald joy too high proclaimed,
And human lips have trembled in God's breath.

O Mother-Maid, thou art ashamed to cover
With thy white self, whereon no stain can be,
Thy God, Who came from Heaven to be thy Lover,
Thy God, Who came from Heaven to dwell in thee.
About thy head celestial legions hover,
Chanting the praise of thy humility.

Magnificat: Annunciation

Noel Rowe

The angel did not draw attention to himself.
He came in. So quietly I could hear

my blood beating on the shore of absolute
beauty. There was fear, yes, but also

faith among familiar things:
light, just letting go the wooden chair,

the breeze, at the doorway, waiting to come in
where, at the table, I prepared a meal,

my knife cutting through the hard skin
of vegetable, hitting wood, and the noise

outside of children playing with their dogs,
throwing him a bone. Then all the sounds

dropped out of hearing. The breeze
drew back, let silence come in first,

and my heart, my heart, was wanting him,
reaching out, and taking hold of smooth-muscled fire.

And it was done. I heard the children laugh
and saw the dog catch the scarred bone.

Ave! Maria!

W. E. B. Du Bois

Ave! Maria!
Mother-maid pitiful
Sister of sorrows
   And daughter of men

Ave! Maria!
Mother of Miracles
Mercy made Wonderful
To thy breast Bountiful
Gather the Sorrowful
   Daughter of Sin

Ave! Maria!
Ave! Maria!
   Gather them in!

The Black Madonna

ALBERT RICE

Not as the white nations
　　know thee,
　　　O Mother!

But swarthy of cheek
　　and full-lipped as the
　　　child races are.

Yet thou art she,
　　the Immaculate Maid,
　　　and none other,

Crowned in the stable
　　at Bethlehem,
　　　hailed of the star.

See where they come,
　　thy people,
　　　so humbly appealing,

From the ancient lands
　　where the olden faiths
　　　had birth.

Tired dusky hands
　　uplifting for thy
　　　healing.

Pity them, Mother,
　　the untaught
　　　of earth.

Mary's Magnificat

HELEN BARRETT MONTGOMERY

Luke 1:47–55

My soul doth magnify the Lord,
My spirit exults in God, who is my Saviour,
For he has regarded the humiliation of his slave,
And from this hour all ages will count me blessed.

For he who is mighty has done great things for me;
And holy is his name.
His mercy is unto generations and generations
On those who reverence him.

He has showed strength with his arm:
He has scattered the proud
    in the imagination of their hearts;
He has put down princes from their thrones,
And has exalted those of low degree.

The hungry he has filled with good things,
But the rich he has sent empty away.
He has helped Israel, his servant,
    that he might remember mercy,
As he spoke to our forefathers,
    to Abraham and his offspring forever.

Those Who Carry

ANNA KAMIENSKA

Those who carry pianos
to the tenth floor wardrobes and coffins
an old man with a bundle of wood limps beyond the horizon
a woman with a hump of nettles
a madwoman pushing a pram
full of vodka bottles
they will all be lifted
like a gull's feather like a dry leaf
like an eggshell a scrap of newspaper

Blessed are those who carry
for they shall be lifted.

The Mother Mary: I

George MacDonald

Mary, to thee the heart was given
   For infant hand to hold,
Thus clasping, an eternal heaven,
   The great earth in its fold.

He seized the world with tender might,
   By making thee his own;
Thee, lowly queen, whose heavenly height
   Was to thyself unknown.

He came, all helpless, to thy power,
   For warmth, and love, and birth;
In thy embraces, every hour,
   He grew into the earth.

And thine the grief, O mother high,
   Which all thy sisters share,
Who keep the gate betwixt the sky
   And this our lower air;

And unshared sorrows, gathering slow,
   New thoughts within the heart,
Which through thee like a sword will go,
   And make thee mourn apart.

For, if a woman bore a son
   That was of angel brood,
Who lifted wings ere day was done,
   And soared from where he stood;

Strange grief would fill each mother-moan,
  Wild longing, dim, and sore:
"My child! my child! he is my own,
  And yet is mine no more!"

And thou, O Mary, years on years,
  From child-birth to the cross,
Wast filled with yearnings, filled with fears,
  Keen sense of love and loss.

His childish thoughts outsoared thy reach;
  His childish tenderness
Had deeper springs than act or speech
  To eye or ear express.

Strange pangs await thee, mother mild!
  A sorer travail-pain,
Before the spirit of thy child
  Is born in thee again.

And thou wilt still forebode and dread,
  And loss be still thy fear,
Till form be gone, and, in its stead,
  The very self appear.

For, when thy Son hath reached his goal,
  His own obedient choice,
Him thou wilt know within thy soul,
  And in his joy rejoice.

III

Behold, Let Us Be Off to Bethlehem
*Poems for Beholding and Remembering
to Linger and Listen*

And Joseph also went up from Galilee,
out of the city of Nazareth, into Judaea,
unto the city of David, which is called Bethlehem;
(because he was of the house and lineage of David)
to be taxed with Mary his espoused wife,
being great with child.

And so it was, that, while they were there,
the days were accomplished that she should be delivered.
And she brought forth her firstborn son,
and wrapped him in swaddling clothes,
and laid him in a manger;
because there was no room for them in the inn.

And there were in the same country
shepherds abiding in the field,
keeping watch over their flock by night.

And, lo,
the angel of the Lord came upon them,
and the glory of the Lord shone round about them:
and they were sore afraid.

And the angel said unto them,
Fear not: for, behold,
I bring you good tidings of great joy,
which shall be to all people.
For unto you is born this day
in the city of David
a Saviour, which is Christ the Lord.
And this shall be a sign unto you;
Ye shall find the babe wrapped in swaddling clothes,
lying in a manger.

And they came with haste,
and found Mary, and Joseph,
and the babe lying in a manger.

From the Gospel According to Luke, chapter 2[1]

You have come to us as a small child,
but you have brought us the greatest of all gifts,
the gift of eternal love.
Caress us with Your tiny hands,
embrace us with Your tiny arms,
and pierce our hearts with Your soft, sweet cries.

Bernard of Clairvaux (1090–1153)

1. King James Version

Make Way

BRENT NEWSOM

Isaiah 40:3–5

This panting land
hawks up roadblocks
over ground hell-bent
against the premise
of a path. Desert
of rock, not dunes.
Hot wind
rattling leaves
of a distant, lone
acacia tree,
scraggly signpost
pointing everyway
into the craggy, cave-
laden wilderness.
Boulders big enough
to cast a shadow
one might shelter in,
or try, in the sun-fried
afternoon. The grade
grows steep
as the valleys deepen
like the dark of death.
Runnels of loosened
smaller rocks where rain
must once have rushed—
rain, in such a place.

What wildness welcomes
a road? What valley
straightens its spine,
what mountain stoops
from its jeweled throne?
But look: a path
flat and straight
through the jagged
crags and ravines.
A route between
two backwaters—
road enough
for a man to walk
beside a donkey,
on which might ride
a woman with child—
from Nazareth away
to Bethlehem. A way.

ADVENT

(On a theme by Dietrich Bonhoeffer)

PAMELA CRANSTON

Look how long
the tired world waited,
locked in its lonely cell,
guilty as a prisoner.

As you can imagine,
it sang and whistled in the dark.
It hoped. It paced and puttered about,
tidying its little piles of inconsequences.

It wept from the weight of ennui
draped like shackles on its wrists.
It raged and wailed against the walls
of its own plight.

But there was nothing
the world could do
to find its freedom.
The door was shut tight.

It could only be opened
from the outside.
Who could believe the latch
would be turned by the flower
of a newborn hand?

The Nativity of Christ

Luis de Góngora

Today from Aurora's bosom
A pink has fallen—a crimson blossom—
And oh, how glorious rests the hay
On which the fallen blossom lay!

When silence gently had unfurled
Her mantle over all below,
And crowned with winter's frost and snow,
Night swayed the sceptre of the world,
Amid the gloom descending slow,
Upon the monarch's frozen bosom
A pink has fallen,—a crimson blossom.

The only flower the Virgin bore
(Aurora fair) within her breast,
She gave to earth, yet still possessed
Her virgin blossom as before;
That hay that colored drop caressed,—
Received upon its faithful bosom
That single flower,—a crimson blossom.

The manger, unto which 'twas given,
Even amid wintry snows and cold,
Within its fostering arms to fold
The blushing flower that fell from heaven,
Was a canopy of gold,—
A downy couch,—where on its bosom
The flower had fallen,—that crimson blossom.

I Saw a Stable

MARY ELIZABETH COLERIDGE

I saw a stable, low and very bare,
A little child in a manger.
The oxen knew Him, had Him in their care,
To men He was a stranger.
The safety of the world was lying there,
And the world's danger.

Let the Stable Still Astonish

Leslie Leyland Fields

Let the stable still astonish:
Straw-dirt floor, dull eyes,
Dusty flanks of donkeys, oxen;
Crumbling, crooked walls;
No bed to carry that pain,
And then, the child,
Rag-wrapped, laid to cry
In a trough.

Who would have chosen this?
Who would have said: "Yes,
Let the God of all the heavens and earth
be born here, in this place."?

Who but the same God
Who stands in the darker, fouler rooms of our hearts
and says, "Yes, let the God
of Heaven and Earth
be born here—

   in this place."

The Shepherd at the Nativity

TANIA RUNYAN

Last night I watched another wet lamb
slide into the dark and beheld this same
drowsy beauty: a mother bending toward
her nursing young. New limbs trembling.
Matching rhythms of breath.

The angels told us to praise and adore.
I spend my life trying not to love
such small things. But again and again
I carry my new lambs and name them,
play songs for them on the reed pipe,
bind their broken legs and search for them
in the foothills, until they are sold and worn,
served up, split open on an altar
and I feel my own blood rushing to the edge.

The Angel at the Nativity

Tania Runyan

Oh, God, I am heavy
with glory. My head thunders
from singing in the hills.

This night will come once.
Enough bright lights.
Enough shouting
at shepherds in the fields.

Let me slip into the stable
and crouch among
the rooting swine.
Let me close my eyes
and feel the child's breath,
this wind that blows
through the mountains and stars,
lifting my weary wings.

Mary at the Nativity

TANIA RUNYAN

The angel said there would be no end
to his kingdom. So for three hundred days
I carried rivers and cedars and mountains.
Stars spilled in my belly when he turned.

Now I can't stop touching his hands,
the pink pebbles of his knuckles,
the soft wrinkle of flesh
between his forefinger and thumb.
I rub his fingernails as we drift
in and out of sleep. They are small
and smooth, like almond petals.
Forever, I will need nothing but these.

But all night, the visitors crowd
around us. I press his palms to my lips
in silence. They look down in anticipation,
as if they expect him to suddenly
spill coins from his hands
or raise a gold scepter
and turn swine into angels.

Isn't this wonder enough
that yesterday he was inside me,
and now he nuzzles next to my heart?
That he wraps his hand around
my finger and holds on?

Joseph at the Nativity

TANIA RUNYAN

Of any birth, I thought this
would be a clean one,
like pulling white linen
from a loom.

But when I return to the cave,
Mary throws her cloak
over the bloody straw and cries.
I know she wants me to leave.

There he lies, stomach rising
and falling, a shriveled pod
that does nothing but stare
at the edge of the feeding trough
with dark, unsteady eyes.

Is he God enough
to know that I am poor,
that we had no time
for a midwife, that swine ate
from his bed this morning?

If the angel was right, he knows.
He knows that Mary's swell
embarrassed me, that I was jealous
of her secret skyward smiles,
that now I want to run into these hills
and never come back.

Peace, peace, I've heard in my dreams.
This child will make you right.

But I can only stand here,
not a husband, not a father,
my hands hanging dumbly
at my sides. Do I touch him,
this child who is mine
and not mine? Do I enter
the kingdom of blood and stars?

I am Joseph

U. A. FANTHORPE

I am Joseph, carpenter,
Of David's kingly line,
I wanted an heir; discovered
My wife's son wasn't mine.

I am an obstinate lover,
Loved Mary for better or worse.
Wouldn't stop loving when I found
Someone Else came first.

Mine was the likeness I hoped for
When the first-born man-child came.
But nothing of him was me. I couldn't
Even choose his name.

I am Joseph, who wanted
To teach my own boy how to live.
My lesson to my foster son:
Endure. Love. Give.

Joseph and Mary

Roscoe Gilmore Stott

Joseph, the simple tradesman, sat nearby,
Awed by his wonder, stilled by sympathy;
Vaguely he mused on what his eyes had seen,
Or pondered slowly what the morn might mean.
Mary slept on—that first blest mother-sleep;
He watched alone; the night was growing deep.
Amazed, he marked new glory flood her face;
Her eyes were closed, but from her lowly place
She called his name, as one who dreams a dream;
And as he came, her face did strangely gleam.
Her arms lay open, and with knowing glance,
He knew he heard her speaking in a trance.

"Look, Joseph, on my Babe—He is King!
Come near and touch my hand; I hear the ring
Of wondrous anthems bursting from the sky;
I am bewildered and I know not why.
Look, sleeps He well? Ah, Joseph, bear with me
In loving patience, as thou hast for we . . .
Joseph, they sing again! Hear ye the choir?
Their faces shine as with a scared fire.
They hover near us—O, a mighty throng
Are singing for my Babe His natal song!
Before His star a thousand stars take flight—
Who placed it there, that wondrous, holy Light? . . .
My joy—dear Joseph, can I bear it all?
My joy!—Ah, see around me fall
The dismal shadows of a distant cross! . . .
My fathers' God, is all this gain or loss?"

And Joseph—for he could not understand—
Knelt by her side and, wondering, kissed her hand.

The Story of the Shepherd

Anonymous Spanish Carol

It was the very noon of night: the stars above the fold,
More sure than clock or chiming bell, the hour of midnight told:
When from the heav'ns there came a voice, and forms were seen to shine
Still bright'ning as the music rose with light and love divine.
With love divine, the song began; there shone a light serene:
O, who hath heard what I have heard, or seen what I have seen?

O ne'er could nightingale at dawn salute the rising day
With sweetness like that bird of song in his immortal lay:
O ne'er were woodnotes heard at eve by banks with poplar shade
So thrilling as the concert sweet by heav'nly harpings made;
For love divine was in each chord, and filled each pause between:
O, who hath heard what I have heard, or seen what I have seen?

I roused me at the piercing strain, but shrunk as from the ray
Of summer lightning: all around so bright the splendour lay.
For oh, it mastered sight and sense, to see that glory shine,
To hear that minstrel in the clouds, who sang of Love Divine,
To see that form with bird-like wings, of more than mortal mien:
O, who hath heard what I have heard, or seen what I have seen?

When once the rapturous trance was past, that so my sense could bind,
I left my sheep to Him whose care breathed in the western wind:
I left them, for instead of snow, I trod on blade and flower,
And ice dissolved in starry rays at morning's gracious hour,
Revealing where on earth the steps of Love Divine had been:
O, who hath heard what I have heard, or seen what I have seen?

I hasted to a low-roofed shed, for so the Angel bade;
And bowed before the lowly rack where Love Divine was laid:
A new-born Babe, like tender Lamb, with Lion's strength there smiled;
For Lion's strength immortal might, was in that new-born Child;
That Love Divine in child-like form had God for ever been:
O, who hath heard what I have heard, or seen what I have seen?

A Shepherd Boy Remembers

Wilda Morris

You ask if I remember
that strange, wondrous night.
How could I forget
the blinding light
as the angel appeared?
I hid my eyes and clung
to my father's robe, thinking
a star had fallen into the field.

The angel's voice was strong
as a ram's, kind as a mother's,
telling us not to be afraid.
How could I forget
the winged choir singing
glory to God, singing of peace
in this world my mother says
is wicked?

I followed father into a stable,
wondering why we'd left our flocks
just to see a new baby cradled
in the oxen's feed trough.
I expected magic to match
the music on the hillside.

The mother saw my confusion,
was tender as a ewe with a newborn lamb
as she motioned me to come closer.
More tender, even, as she touched

the baby's toes, his dimpled chin,
and invited me to touch his cheek.
It was cool and smooth
as a pebble from a running stream.

The angels' song bounced around in my head,
peace, peace, like my father's flute
echoing in the hills. I only partly
understood. Still, I slept, unafraid,
as father carried me home,
humming his own expectation
of peace.

The Shepherd Who Stayed

Theodosia Garrison

There are in Paradise
Souls neither great nor wise,
Yet souls who wear no less
The crown of faithfulness.

My master bade me watch the flock by night;
My duty was to stay. I do not know
What thing my comrades saw in that great light,
I did not heed the words that bade them go,
I know not were they maddened or afraid;
    I only know I stayed.

The hillside seemed on fire; I felt the sweep
Of wings above my head; I ran to see
If any danger threatened these my sheep.
What though I found them folded quietly,
What though my brother wept and plucked my sleeve,
    They were not mine to leave.

Thieves in the wood and wolves upon the hill,
My duty was to stay. Strange though it be,
I had no thought to hold my mates, no will
To bid them wait and keep the watch with me.
I had not heard that summons they obeyed;
    I only know I stayed.

Perchance they will return upon the dawn
With word of Bethlehem and why they went.

I only know that watching here alone,
I know a strange content.
I have not failed that trust upon me laid;
I ask no more—I stayed.

Lullaby: Sanctus Deus

U. A. FANTHORPE

(for Jessica Weeks)

The Angels

Sanctus deus, sleep.
Careful angels keep
Watch from sky's vast sweep.
Nothing moves but sheep.
Lord of heaven, sanctus deus,
Now's the time for sleep.

Mary and Joseph

Baby Jesus, dream
Of some happy theme.
Toothless darling, beam;
Here's no cause to scream.
Mary, Joseph, novice parents,
Whisper: *Baby, dream.*

The Ox

Little man-calf, grow.
You have far to go.
I, the patient, slow,
Stable ox, say so.
Lord of heaven, little calf-man,
My advice is: *Grow.*

What the Donkey Saw

U. A. FANTHORPE

No room in the inn, of course,
And not that much in the stable,
What with the shepherds, Magi, Mary,
Joseph, the heavenly host—
Not to mention the baby
Using our manger as a cot.
You couldn't have squeezed another cherub in
For love nor money.

Still, in spite of the overcrowding,
I did my best to make them feel wanted.
I could see the baby and I
Would be going places together.

A Christmas Prayer

George MacDonald

Loving looks the large-eyed cow,
Loving stares the long-eared ass
At Heaven's glory in the grass!
Child, with added human birth
Come to bring the child of earth
Glad repentance, tearful mirth,
And a seat beside the hearth
At the Father's knee—
Make us peaceful as thy cow;
Make us patient as thine ass;
Make us quiet as thou art now;
Make us strong as thou wilt be.
Make us always know and see
We are his as well as thou.

The Wicked Fairy at the Manger

U. A. FANTHORPE

My gift for the child:

No wife, kids, home;
No money sense. Unemployable.
Friends, yes. But the wrong sort—
The workshy, women, wogs,
Petty infringers of the law, persons
With notifiable diseases,
Poll tax collectors, tarts,
The bottom rung.

      His end?
I think we'll make it
Public, prolonged, painful.

Right, said the baby. *That was roughly*
What we had in mind.

The Innkeeper's Regrets

Wilda Morris

I was suspicious of those travelers from Nazareth—
all my life I'd been taught that no good
could come from there, and my inn
was full when those peasants knocked. Despite
my disdain, I took pity on the weary young woman,
heavy with child and her husband
with callused hands and tired feet.
The space I offered in the stable
was surely better than giving birth
on a dusty road or beneath a tree.

I thought myself generous but now I blush
at my paltry pity and how I thought peasants
are best hosted with braying donkeys,
best bedded down with oxen,
that a peasant mother should be satisfied
with straw-filled manger as a baby bed.

Now I ask my wife, *Why didn't you
take them hot barley soup
and fresh-baked bread? Why didn't you
offer them our own bed?* Even as I ask,
I know I'm excusing myself,
passing blame for my blunder.
As I pray with penitence,
I promise compassion instead of pity
for those who need my help.
I will look for the divine in every face,
even weary wayfarers from Nazareth.

How the Natal Star was Born

VIOLET NESDOLY

The Son vanishes just after I am sent
to the Galilean virgin
and heaven isn't the same.
Gone the laughter, mischief, hijinks.
Music replaced by silence
all monochromatic, sober
like the life of the party has left
and we don't have the will
to keep partying or to go home.

The Almighty's been moody since then
broods like never before
over calendars and seasons
looks down a lot, mostly toward Nazareth
at this blossoming virgin-still
and her earthmate.

The day this couple sets off down the road
He starts pacing pacing   pacing
When they get to Bethlehem
it's pace-pace-pace
then He pauses   *Hush!*

All the hosts of heaven stop their chatter
crowd behind Abraham, Isaac, Jacob, David
peer over the balcony
focus on a dark building
near a sign that blinks *Sorry—No Vacancy.*
It's so quiet you can hear the stars hum.

Then cutting the night
tiny and tremulous
A-wah a-wah a-wah a-wah

The Almighty laughs His magnificence
tosses His glory, flings His radiance
and then starts handing out
cig—no, trumpets
to every angel within arm's reach
Go tell somebody, anybody!

After they've left He asks for the bubbly
shakes it up
pops the cork
sprays it all over heaven.

Two Carols

Evelyn Underhill

Flores apparuerunt in terra nostra

Very still was all the land,
    Very secret was the hour;
Darkness as a guard did stand
    When the Rose brought forth the flower—
      Rosa sine spina.

Long the road and hard the pain,
    Chill and lowly was the shed:
See, upon the straw she's lain—
    Straw, to make her childing-bed!
      Virgo et regina.

Cold the welcome, sharp the smart;
    Godhead treads the bitter way.
Only in the lowly heart
    Is her Babe brought forth today—
      Genetrix divina.

II
Omnis creatura ingemiscit, et parturit usque adhuc.

Silence and darkness! land and sea
    Await the ending of their pain.
Qui est in coelis now shall be
    One with the world he made again.
        Dominus tecum!
        So the angels say,
        So may it be alway!

Poor Earth, that hast in exile long
    Borne alien gods, thy travail cease!
Lift up, lift up, the mother's song:
    Rex natus est, his name is Peace.
          Dominus tecum!
          So the angels say,
          So may it be alway!

Adveniat regnum! in the heart
    Love's childing-bed is made to-night.
There is he born that heals thy smart,
    Emmanuel, the Light of Light!
          Dominus tecum!
          So the angels say,
          So may it be alway![1]

1. *Flores apparuerunt in terra nostra*: the flowers appear on the earth, Song of Solomon 2:12

Rosa sine spina: a dazzling rose without a thorn

Virgo et regina: Queen of virgins

Genetrix divina: Mother of grace

Omnis creatura ingemiscit, et parturit usque adhuc:All creation has been groaning in travail together until now, Romans 8:22

Qui est in coelis: Who is in heaven

Dominus tecum!: The Lord is with thee!

Rex natus est: King is born

Adveniat regnum!: Thy Kingdom come!

The Christmas Silence

Margaret Deland

Hushed are the pigeons cooing low,
On dusty rafters of the loft;
And mild-eyed oxen, breathing soft,
Sleep on the fragrant hay below.

Dim shadows in the corner hide;
The glimmering lantern's rays are shed
Where one young lamb just lifts his head,
Then huddles 'gainst his mother's side.

Strange silence tingles in the air;
Through the half-open door a bar
Of light from one low hanging star
Touches a baby's radiant hair—

No sound—the mother, kneeling, lays
Her cheek against the little face.
Oh human love! Oh heavenly grace!
'Tis yet in silence that she prays!

Ages of silence end to-night;
Then to the long-expectant earth
Glad angels come to greet His birth
In burst of music, love, and light!

A Song of the Virgin Mother

Lope de Vega

As ye go through these palm-trees
O holy angel;
Sith sleepeth my child here
Still ye the branches.

O Bethlehem palm-trees
That move to the anger
Of winds in their fury,
Tempestuous voices,
Make ye no clamour,
Run ye less swiftly,
Sith sleepeth the child here
Still ye the branches.

He the divine child
Is here a-wearied
Of weeping the earth-pain,
Here for his rest would he
Cease from his mourning,
Only a little while,
Sith sleepeth this child here
Stay ye the branches.

Cold be the fierce winds,
Treacherous round him.
Ye see that I have not
Wherewith to guard him,
O angels, divine ones

That pass us a-flying,
Sith sleepeth my child here
Stay ye the branches.

In the Carpenter's Shop

SARA TEASDALE

Mary sat in the corner dreaming,
Dim was the room and low,
While in the dusk, the saw went screaming
To and fro.

Jesus and Joseph toiled together,
Mary was watching them,
Thinking of kings in the wintry weather
At Bethlehem.

Mary sat in the corner thinking,
Jesus had grown a man;
One by one her hopes were sinking
As the years ran.

Jesus and Joseph toiled together,
Mary's thoughts were far
Angels sang in the wintry weather
Under a star.

Mary sat in the corner weeping,
Bitter and hot her tears
Little faith were the angels keeping
All the years.

IV

Behold, Magi from the East Arrived
*Poems for Beholding and Remembering
the Gift of Starlight and Strangers*

Jesus was born at Bethlehem in Judea during the reign of Herod.
After his birth magi from the east arrived in Jerusalem, asking,
> *Where is the child*
> *who is born to be king of the Jews?*
> *We observed the rising of his star,*
> *and we have come to pay him homage.*

King Herod was greatly perturbed when he heard this;
> and so was the whole of Jerusalem.

Herod called the magi to meet him in private,
> then he sent them on to Bethlehem, and said,
> > *Go and make a careful inquiry for the child.*
> > *When you have found him, report to me,*
> > *so that I may go myself and pay him homage.*

They set out at Herod's bidding;
> and the star
> which they had seen at its rising
> went ahead of them
> until it stopped above the place where the child lay.

At the sight of the star they were overjoyed.
Entering the house,
> they saw the child with Mary his mother,
> and bowed to the ground in homage to him.

Then they opened their treasures and offered him gifts:

gold, frankincense, and myrrh.
And being warned in a dream
  not to go back to Herod,
  they returned home another way.

From The Gospel According to Matthew, chapter 2[1]

Almighty and everlasting God,
  who hast made known the Incarnation of Thy Son
    by the bright shining of a star,
      which, when the magi beheld,
        they presented costly gifts and adored Thy Majesty;
grant that the star of Thy Righteousness
  may always shine into our hearts;
    and that, as our treasure,
      we may give ourselves and all we possess to Thy service.

Gelasian Sacramentary, 494 AD

1. The New English Bible

Far Across the Desert Floor

GEORGE MACDONALD

(A portion of "An Old Story")

Far across the desert floor,
Come, slow-drawing nigher,
Sages deep in starry lore,
Priests of burning Fire.
In the sky they read his story.
And, through starlight cool,
They come riding to the Glory,
To the Wonderful.

Babe and mother, coming Mage,
Shepherd, ass, and cow!
Angels watching the new age,
Time's intensest Now!
Heaven down-brooding, Earth upstraining,
Far ends closing in!
Sure the eternal tide is gaining
On the strand of sin!

See! but see! Heaven's chapel-master
Signs with lifted hand;
Winds divine blow fast and faster,
Swelling bosoms grand.
Hark the torrent-joy let slip!
Hark the great throats ring!
Glory! Peace! Good-fellowship!
And a Child for king!

Star Silver

CARL SANDBURG

The silver of one star
Plays cross-lights against pine green.

And the play of this silver
crosswise against the green
Is an old story ...
                    thousands of years.

And sheep raisers on the hills by night
Watching the wooly four-footed ramblers,
Watching a single silver star—
Why does the story never wear out?

And a baby slung in a feed-box
Back in a barn in a Bethlehem slum,
A baby's first cry mixing with the crunch
Of a mule's teeth on Bethlehem Christmas corn,
Baby fists softer than snowflakes of Norway,
The vagabond Mother of Christ
And the vagabond men of wisdom,
All in a barn on a winter night,
And a baby there in swaddling clothes on hay—
Why does the story never wear out?

The sheen of it all
Is a star silver and a pine green
For the heart of a child asking a story,
The red and hungry, red and hankering heart
Calling for cross-lights of silver and green.

Christmastide

EMILY PAULINE JOHNSON
(TEKAHIONWAKE)

I may not go to-night to Bethlehem,
Nor follow star-directed ways, nor tread
The paths wherein the shepherds walked, that led
To Christ, and peace, and God's good will to men.

I may not hear the Herald Angel's song
Peal through the Oriental skies, nor see
The wonder of that Heavenly company
Announce the King the world had waited long.

The manger throne I may not kneel before,
Or see how man to God is reconciled,
Through pure St. Mary's purer, holier child;
The human Christ these eyes may not adore.

I may not carry frankincense and myrrh
With adoration to the Holy One;
Nor gold have I to give the Perfect Son,
To be with those wise kings a worshipper.

Not mine the joy that Heaven sent to them,
For ages since Time swung and locked his gates,
But I may kneel without—the star still waits
To guide me on to holy Bethlehem.

Nativity

SCOTT CAIRNS

As you lean in, you'll surely apprehend
the tiny God is wrapped
in something more than swaddle. The God

is tightly bound within
His blesséd mother's gaze—her face declares
that she is rapt by what

she holds, beholds, reclines beholden to.
She cups His perfect head
and kisses Him, that even here the radiant

compass of affection
is announced, that even here our several
histories converge and slip,

just briefly, out of time. Which is much of what
an icon works as well,
and this one offers up a broad array

of separate narratives
whose temporal relations quite miss the point,
or meet there. Regardless,

one blithe shepherd offers music to the flock,
and—just behind him—there
he is again, and sore afraid, attended

by a trembling companion
and addressed by Gabriel. Across the ridge,
three wise men spur three horses

towards a star, and bowing at the icon's
nearest edge, these same three
yet adore the seated One whose mother serves

as throne. Meantime, stumped,
the kindly Abba Joseph ruminates,
receiving consolation

from an attentive dog whose master may
yet prove to be a holy
messenger disguised as fool. Overhead,

the famous star is all
but out of sight by now; yet, even so,
it aims a single ray

directing our slow pilgrims to the core
where all the journeys meet,
appalling crux and hallowed cave and womb,

where crouched among these other
lowing cattle at their trough, our travelers
receive that creatured air, and pray.

Christmas Eve at Sea

John Masefield

A wind is rustling "south and soft,"
  Cooing a quiet country tune,
The calm sea sighs, and far aloft
  The sails are ghostly in the moon.

Unquiet ripples lisp and purr,
  A block there pipes and chirps i' the sheave,
The wheel-ropes jar, the reef-points stir
  Faintly—and it is Christmas Eve.

The hushed sea seems to hold her breath;
  And o'er the giddy, swaying spars,
Silent and excellent as Death,
  The dim blue skies are bright with stars.

Dear God—they shone in Palestine
  Like this, and yon pale moon serene
Looked down among the lowing kine
  On Mary and the Nazarene.

The angels called from deep to deep,
  The burning heavens felt the thrill,
Startling the flocks of silly sheep
  And lonely shepherds on the hill.

To-night beneath the dripping bows
  Where flashing bubbles burst and throng,
The bow-wash murmurs and sighs and soughs
  A message from the angels' song.

The moon goes nodding down the west,
    The drowsy helmsman strikes the bell;
Rex Judaeorum natus est,[1]
    I charge you, brothers, sing *Nowell, Nowell,*
Rex Judaeorum natus est.

1. *Rex Judaeorum natus est:* Newborn King of the Jews.

Huron Carol

JEAN DE BRÉBEUF

'Twas in the moon of winter-time
When all the birds had fled,
That mighty Gitchi Manitou
Sent angel choirs instead;
Before their light the stars grew dim,
And wandering hunters heard the hymn:
"Jesus your King is born, Jesus is born,
In excelsis gloria."

Within a lodge of broken bark
The tender Babe was found,
A ragged robe of rabbit skin
Enwrapp'd His beauty round;
But as the hunter braves drew nigh,
The angel song rang loud and high . . .
"Jesus your King is born, Jesus is born,
In excelsis gloria."

The earliest moon of wintertime
Is not so round and fair
As was the ring of glory
On the helpless infant there.
The chiefs from far before him knelt
With gifts of fox and beaver pelt.
"Jesus your King is born, Jesus is born,
In excelsis gloria."

O children of the forest free,
O sons of Manitou,
The Holy Child of earth and heaven
Is born today for you.
Come kneel before the radiant Boy
Who brings you beauty, peace and joy.
"Jesus your King is born, Jesus is born,
In excelsis gloria."

Christmas Carol

SARA TEASDALE

The kings they came from out the south,
　　All dressed in ermine fine;
They bore Him gold and chrysoprase,
　　And gifts of precious wine.

The shepherds came from out the north,
　　Their coats were brown and old;
They brought Him little new-born lambs—
　　They had not any gold.

The wise men came from out the east,
　　And they were wrapped in white;
The star that led them all the way
　　Did glorify the night.

The angels came from heaven high,
　　And they were clad with wings;
And lo, they brought a joyful song
　　The host of heaven sings.

The kings they knocked upon the door,
　　The wise men entered in,
The shepherds followed after them
　　To hear the song begin.

The angels sang through all the night
　　Until the rising sun,
But little Jesus fell asleep
　　Before the song was done.

The Magi

WILLIAM BUTLER YEATS

Now as at all times I can see in the mind's eye,
In their stiff, painted clothes, the pale unsatisfied ones
Appear and disappear in the blue depths of the sky
With all their ancient faces like rain-beaten stones,
And all their helms of silver hovering side by side,
And all their eyes still fixed, hoping to find once more,
Being by Calvary's turbulence unsatisfied,
The uncontrollable mystery on the bestial floor.

The Child in the Manger

SUSAN LANGSTAFF MITCHELL

His presence set the skies aflame,
As through the glittering zones He came,
The Heavenly Child as He swept by,
Snatched one bright bauble from the sky.
The Magi watched the heavens afar,
Saw in the blue a starry stranger.
But He whose playthings planets are,
Lay innocently in the manger.

The Star of the Heart

SUSAN LANGSTAFF MITCHELL

The Star has risen in the heart,
The sweet light flushes every part.
The shepherds of the body know,
The rumour reached them long ago,
Abiding in the fields were they
When Deity informed the clay.
The wise kings of the mind bow down,
They yield the Wiser King His crown;
Before a cradle they unfold
The myrrh and frankincense and gold.

Nativity

John Donne

Immensity cloistered in thy dear womb,
Now leaves His well-belov'd imprisonment,
There He hath made Himself to His intent
Weak enough, now into the world to come;
But O, for thee, for Him, hath the inn no room?
Yet lay Him in this stall, and from the Orient,
Stars and wise men will travel to prevent
The effect of Herod's jealous general doom.
Seest thou, my soul, with thy faith's eyes, how He
Which fills all place, yet none holds Him, doth lie?
Was not His pity towards thee wondrous high,
That would have need to be pitied by thee?
Kiss Him, and with Him into Egypt go,
With His kind mother, who partakes thy woe.

A Christmas Carol

George MacDonald

Babe Jesus lay in Mary's lap,
　　The sun shone in his hair;
And this was how she saw, mayhap,
　　The crown already there.

For she sang: "Sleep on, my little king;
　　Bad Herod dares not come;
Before thee sleeping, holy thing,
　　The wild winds would be dumb."

"I kiss thy hands, I kiss thy feet,
　　My child, so long desired;
Thy hands will never be soiled, my sweet;
　　Thy feet will never be tired."

"For thou art the king of men, my son;
　　Thy crown I see it plain!
And men shall worship thee, every one,
　　And cry, Glory! Amen!"

Babe Jesus he opened his eyes wide—
　　At Mary looked her lord.
Mother Mary stinted her song and sighed;
　　Babe Jesus said never a word.

The Three Kings

HENRY WADSWORTH LONGFELLOW

Three Kings came riding from far away,
   Melchior and Gaspar and Baltasar;
Three Wise Men out of the East were they.
And they travelled by night and they slept by day
   For their guide was a beautiful, wonderful star.

The star was so beautiful, large, and clear,
   That all the other stars of the sky
Became a white mist in the atmosphere,
And by this they knew that the coming was near
   Of the Prince foretold in the prophecy.

Three caskets they bore on their saddlebows,
   Three caskets of gold with golden keys;
Their robes were of crimson silk with rows
Of bells and pomegranates and furbelows,
   Their turbans like blossoming almond-trees.

And so the Three Kings rode into the West,
   Through the dusk of night, over hill and dell,
And sometimes they nodded with beard on breast,
And sometimes talked, as they paused to rest,
   With the people they met at some wayside well.

"Of the child that is born," said Baltasar,
   "Good people, I pray you, tell us the news;
For we in the East have seen his star,
And have ridden fast, and have ridden far,
   To find and worship the King of the Jews."

And the people answered, "You ask in vain;
  We know of no king but Herod the Great!"
They thought the Wise Men were men insane,
As they spurred their horses across the plain,
  Like riders in haste, and who cannot wait.

And when they came to Jerusalem,
  Herod the Great, who had heard this thing,
Sent for the Wise Men and questioned them;
And said, "Go down unto Bethlehem,
  And bring me tidings of this new king."

So they rode away; and the star stood still,
  The only one in the gray of morn;
Yes, it stopped,—it stood still of its own free will,
Right over Bethlehem on the hill,
  The city of David where Christ was born.

And the Three Kings rode through the gate and the guard,
  Through the silent street, till their horses turned
And neighed as they entered the great inn yard;
But the windows were closed, and the doors were barred,
  And only a light in the stable burned.

And cradled there in the scented hay,
  In the air made sweet by the breath of kine,
The little child in the manger lay,
The child, that would be king one day
  Of a kingdom not human but divine.

His mother Mary of Nazareth
  Sat watching beside his place of rest,
Watching the even flow of his breath,
For the joy of life and the terror of death
  Were mingled together in her breast.

They laid their offerings at his feet:
  The gold was their tribute to a King,
The frankincense, with its odor sweet,
Was for the Priest, the Paraclete,
  The myrrh for the body's burying.

And the mother wondered and bowed her head,
    And sat as still as a statue of stone;
Her heart was troubled yet comforted,
Remembering what the Angel had said
    Of an endless reign and of David's throne.

Then the Kings rode out of the city gate,
    With a clatter of hoofs in proud array;
But they went not back to Herod the Great,
For they knew his malice and feared his hate,
    And returned to their homes by another way.

No Country for Two Kings

LESLIE LEYLAND FIELDS

A king has come. There is no bed
in hostel or heart for a girl
bursting with child. No bed
for a birth no matter how
infant or Hebrew he is,
no matter how long
the signs for his coming. See,
there he lies among dung
and black sheep in a two-mule town:
This is no place for a king.

But Herod hears. If you're the solo royal
any rumor of a rival is good enough to
make the mad exchange:
a thousand babies dying for his crown,
a thousand mothers wailing for grief
    for his relief.
This is no country for two kings.

And when the child grows up crude
with tools and wood, yet dares to rule
over sickness, greed and fear,
he wins a timbered throne, is crowned
with thorns and irony—

The signs are clear:
this is how kings are kept,
   how man redeems:
Yes, let all the children die for me,
while another lifts his bleeding head,
Let me die to make my children royalty.

A Ballad for the Wise Men

MARGARET WIDDEMER

The Christ-Child lay in Bethlehem
    And the Wise Men gave Him gold,
And Mary-Mother she hearkened them
    As they prayed in the cattle-fold:
"Smile then, smile, little Prince of Earth,
    Smile in Thy holy sleep,
Now Thou art come, for want and dearth
There shall be plenty and light and mirth
    Through lands where the poor folk weep."
But Mary-Mother was still and pale
    And she raised her golden-ringed head,
"Then why have I heard the children wail
All night long on the far-blown gale
    While my own Child slept?" she said.
(But far overhead the angels sang:
"There shall be joy!" the clear notes rang!)

The Christ-Child lay in Bethlehem
    And the censers burned for him
That the Wise Men swung on its silver stem
    And prayed while the smoke rose dim:
"Sleep, then sleep, little Son of God,
    Sleep while the whole world prays;
All the world shall fear Thy nod,
Following close Thy staff and rod,
    Praising this day of days."
But Mary-Mother turned whispering
    There by the manger-bed

"Then why do I hear the mocking ring
Of voices crying and questioning
    Through the scented smoke?" she said.
(But high overhead the angels sang–
"There shall be faith!" the pure notes rang.)

The Christ-Child lay in Bethlehem
    And the Wise Men gave Him myrrh,
And Mary-Mother she hearkened them
    As they prayed by the heart of her:
"Sleep, then sleep, little Prince of Peace,
    Sleep, take Thy holy rest,
Now Thou art come all wars shall cease,
Thou who hast brought all strife release
    Even from east to west!"
But Mary-Mother she veiled her head
    As if her great joys were lost,
And "Here is only a manger-bed,
Then why do I hear clashed swords?" she said.
"And why do I see the tide of red
    Over the whole world tossed?"
(But still overhead the angels sang:
"There shall be peace!" the sure notes rang!)

The Gift

WILLIAM CARLOS WILLIAMS

As the wise men of old brought gifts
    guided by a star
        to the humble birthplace
of the god of love,
    the devils
        as an old print shows
retreated in confusion.
    What could a baby know
        of gold ornaments
or frankincense and myrrh,
    of priestly robes
        and devout genuflections?
But the imagination
    knows all stories
        before they are told
and knows the truth of this one
    past all defection.
The rich gifts
    so unsuitable for a child
        though devoutly proffered,
stood for all that love can bring.
    The men were old
        how could they know
of a mother's needs
    or a child's
        appetite?

But as they kneeled
    the child was fed.
        They saw it
and
    gave praise!
        A miracle
had taken place,
    hard gold to love,
a mother's milk!
    before
        their wondering eyes.
The ass brayed
    the cattle lowed.
        It was their nature.
All men by their nature give praise.
    It is all
        they can do.
The very devils
    by their flight give praise.
        What is death,
beside this?
    Nothing. The wise men
        came with gift
and bowed down
    to worship
        this perfection.

When Giving Is All We Have

ALBERTO RIOS

> *One river gives*
> *Its journey to the next.*

We give because someone gave to us.
We give because nobody gave to us.

We give because giving has changed us.
We give because giving could have changed us.

We have been better for it,
We have been wounded by it—

Giving has many faces: It is loud and quiet,
Big, though small, diamond in wood-nails.

Its story is old, the plot worn and the pages too,
But we read this book, anyway, over and again:

Giving is, first and every time, hand to hand,
Mine to yours, yours to mine.

You gave me blue and I gave you yellow.
Together we are simple green. You gave me

What you did not have, and I gave you
What I had to give—together, we made

Something greater from the difference.

Promise

GEORGIA DOUGLAS JOHNSON

Through the moil and the gloom they have issued
    To the steps of the unwinding hill,
Where the sweet, dulcet pipes of tomorrow
    In their preluding rhapsodies trill.

With a thud comes a stir in the bosom,
    As there steals on the sight from afar,
Through a break of a cloud's coiling shadow
    The gleam of a bright morning star!

V

Behold, Ye Bells; Be Joyful, All

*Poems for Beholding and Remembering
to Wake and Worship and Rejoice*

And suddenly
there was with the angel
a multitude of the heavenly host
praising God, and saying,
> *Glory to God in the highest,*
> *and on earth peace, good will toward men.*

And it came to pass,
as the angels were gone away from them into heaven,
the shepherds said one to another,
> *Let us now go even unto Bethlehem,*
> *and see this thing which is come to pass,*
> *which the Lord hath made known unto us.*

And when they had seen it,
they made known abroad
the saying which was made known to them
concerning this child,
and all they that heard it wondered at these things
which were told them by the shepherds.
And the shepherds returned,
glorifying and praising God

for all the things
that they had heard and seen,
as it was told unto them.

from the Gospel According to Luke, chapter 2[1]

Thou shalt know Him when He comes
Not by any din of drums
Nor by the vantage of His airs
Nor by anything He wears—
Neither by His crown—
Nor His gown—
For His Presence known shall be
By the Holy Harmony
That His coming makes in thee.

Unknown 15th century writer

1. King James Version

Christmas Carol

PAUL LAURENCE DUNBAR

Ring out, ye bells!
All Nature swells
With gladness at the wondrous story,—
The world was lorn,
But Christ is born
To change our sadness into glory.

Sing, earthlings, sing!
To-night a King
Hath come from heaven's high throne to bless us.
The outstretched hand
O'er all the land
Is raised in pity to caress us.

Come at his call;
Be joyful all;
Away with mourning and with sadness!
The heavenly choir
With holy fire
Their voices raise in songs of gladness.

The darkness breaks
And Dawn awakes,
Her cheeks suffused with youthful blushes.
The rocks and stones
In holy tones
Are singing sweeter than the thrushes.

Then why should we
In silence be,
When Nature lends her voice to praises;
When heaven and earth
Proclaim the truth
Of Him for whom that lone star blazes?

No, be not still,
But with a will
Strike all your harps and set them ringing;
On hill and heath
Let every breath
Throw all its power into singing!

A Christmas Carol

Robert Herrick

Sung to the King in the Presence at White-Hall

What sweeter music can we bring,
Than a carol, for to sing
The birth of this our heavenly King?
Awake the voice! Awake the string!
Heart, ear, and eye, and everything.
Awake! the while the active finger
Runs division with the singer.

Dark and dull night, fly hence away,
And give the honor to this day,
That sees December turned to May.

If we may ask the reason, say
The why, and wherefore, all things here
Seem like the springtime of the year?

Why does the chilling Winter's morn
Smile, like a field beset with corn?
Or smell, like to a mead new-shorn,
Thus, on the sudden?

Come and see
The cause, why things thus fragrant be:
'Tis He is born, whose quickening birth
Gives life and luster, public mirth,
To heaven, and the under-earth.

We see Him come, and know Him ours,
Who, with His sunshine, and His showers,
Turns all the patient ground to flowers.

The Darling of the world is come,
And fit it is, we find a room
To welcome Him. The nobler part
Of all the house here, is the heart,

Which we will give Him; and bequeath
This holly, and this ivy wreath,
To do Him honor; who's our King,
And Lord of all this reveling.

Ring Out, Wild Bells

Alfred, Lord Tennyson

Ring out, wild bells, to the wild sky,
    The flying cloud, the frosty light:
    The year is dying in the night;
Ring out, wild bells, and let him die.

Ring out the old, ring in the new,
    Ring, happy bells, across the snow:
    The year is going, let him go;
Ring out the false, ring in the true.

Ring out the grief that saps the mind
    For those that here we see no more;
    Ring out the feud of rich and poor,
Ring in redress to all mankind.

Ring out a slowly dying cause,
    And ancient forms of party strife;
    Ring in the nobler modes of life,
With sweeter manners, purer laws.

Ring out the want, the care, the sin,
    The faithless coldness of the times;
    Ring out, ring out my mournful rhymes
But ring the fuller minstrel in.

Ring out false pride in place and blood,
    The civic slander and the spite;
    Ring in the love of truth and right,
Ring in the common love of good.

Ring out old shapes of foul disease;
Ring out the narrowing lust of gold;
Ring out the thousand wars of old,
Ring in the thousand years of peace.

Ring in the valiant man and free,
The larger heart, the kindlier hand;
Ring out the darkness of the land,
Ring in the Christ that is to be.

Christmas

GEORGE HERBERT

I
After all pleasures as I rid one day,
    My horse and I, both tired, body and mind,
    With full cry of affections, quite astray;
I took up the next inn I could find.

There when I came, whom found I but my dear,
    My dearest Lord, expecting till the grief
    Of pleasures brought me to Him, ready there
To be all passengers' most sweet relief?

Oh Thou, whose glorious, yet contracted light,
    Wrapt in night's mantle, stole into a manger;
    Since my dark soul and brutish is Thy right,
To man of all beasts be not Thou a stranger:

    Furnish and deck my soul, that Thou mayst have
    A better lodging, than a rack, or grave.

II
The shepherds sing; and shall I silent be?
    My God, no hymn for Thee?
My soul's a shepherd too; a flock it feeds
    Of thoughts, and words, and deeds.
The pasture is Thy word: the streams, Thy grace
    Enriching all the place.
Shepherd and flock shall sing, and all my powers
    Outsing the daylight hours.

Then will we chide the sun for letting night
    Take up his place and right:
We sing one common Lord; wherefore he should
    Himself the candle hold.
I will go searching, till I find a sun
    Shall stay, till we have done;
A willing shiner, that shall shine as gladly,
    As frost-nipped suns look sadly.
Then will we sing, and shine all our own day,
    And one another pay:
His beams shall cheer my breast, and both so twine,
Till ev'n His beams sing, and my music shine.

Christmas

Toru Dutt

The sky is dark, the snow descends,
    Ring bells, ring out your merriest chime!
Jesus is born; the Virgin bends
    Above Him. O the happy time!

No curtains bright-festooned are hung,
    To shield the Infant from the cold;
The spider-webs alone are slung
    Upon the rafters bare and old.

On fresh straw lies the little One,
    Not in a palace, but a farm,
And kindly oxen breathe upon
    His manger-bed to keep it warm.

White wreaths of snow the roofs attire,
    And o'er them stars the blue adorn,
And hark! In white the angel-quire
    Sing to the Shepherds, "Christ is born."

Noel: Christmas Eve 1913

ROBERT BRIDGES

Pax hominibus bonae voluntatis

A frosty Christmas Eve
    when the stars were shining
Fared I forth alone
    where westward falls the hill,
And from many a village
    in the water'd valley
Distant music reach'd me
    peals of bells a-ringing:
The constellated sounds
    ran sprinkling on earth's floor
As the dark vault above
    with stars was spangled o'er.

Then sped my thoughts to keep
    that first Christmas of all
When the shepherds watching
    by their folds ere the dawn
Heard music in the fields
    and marveling could not tell
Whether it were angels
    or the bright stars singing.

Now blessed be the tow'rs
    that crown England so fair
That stand up strong in prayer
    unto God for our souls

Blessed be their founders
        (said I) and our country folk
Who are ringing for Christ
        in the belfries to-night
With arms lifted to clutch
        the rattling ropes that race
Into the dark above
        and the mad romping din.

But to me heard afar
        it was heav'nly music
Angels' song, comforting
        as the comfort of Christ
When he spake tenderly
        to his sorrowful flock:
The old words came to me
        by the riches of time
Mellow'd and transfigured
        as I stood on the hill
Heark'ning in the aspect
        of th' eternal silence.[1]

1. *Pax hominibus bonae voluntatis:* and peace on earth to men of goodwill

Harness Bells

TED KOOSER

Though the quieter, snow-softened days
of the sleigh horse were then only four or five
decades behind us, our uncle's short strap
of harness bells looked very old, the leather
brown as a mummy, dried and curled up
at the cut ends. There must have been eight
or ten of them, cast from brass, about the size
of a walnut, fastened a couple of inches apart,
each shaped like a hand cupping a baseball,
getting ready to throw it, a clear, watery ball
of bright ringing. You've seen plenty of bells
of that shape, although smaller and lighter,
a few clustered over a shop door to tinkle,
announcing your entrance. But these bells
were heavy with family tradition: Supper,
Christmas Eves in the war years, my uncle
lifting them out of his Ford's trunk, then
thunking it closed, that sound part of it, too,
our fat bachelor uncle, making merry,
jingling them over the snow to our door.

Music on Christmas Morning

ANNE BRONTË

Music I love—but never strain
Could kindle raptures so divine,
So grief assuage, so conquer pain,
And rouse this pensive heart of mine—
As that we hear on Christmas morn,
Upon the wintry breezes born.

Though Darkness still her empire keep,
And hours must pass, ere morning break;
From troubled dreams, or slumbers deep,
That music kindly bids us wake:
It calls us, with an angel's voice,
To wake, and worship, and rejoice;

To greet with joy the glorious morn,
Which angels welcomed long ago,
When our redeeming Lord was born,
To bring the light of Heaven below;
The Powers of Darkness to dispel,
And rescue Earth from Death and Hell.

While listening to that sacred strain,
My raptured spirit soars on high;
I seem to hear those songs again
Resounding through the open sky,
That kindled such divine delight,
In those who watched their flocks by night.

With them—I celebrate His birth—
Glory to God, in highest Heaven,
Good will to men, and peace on Earth,
To us a Saviour-king is given;
Our God is come to claim His own,
And Satan's power is overthrown!

A sinless God, for sinful men,
Descends to suffer and to bleed;
Hell must renounce its empire then;
The price is paid, the world is freed.
And Satan's self must now confess,
That Christ has earned a Right to bless:

Now holy Peace may smile from heaven,
And heavenly Truth from earth shall spring:
The captive's galling bonds are riven,
For our Redeemer is our king;
And He that gave his blood for men
Will lead us home to God again.

Christmas Morn

ANNA DE BRÉMONT

There's a holy light like a beacon bright,
    Afar over land and sea.
Soft its lambent ray o'er the broad earth plays
    With a rosy dancing glee,
And the topmost peak of the mountains bleak
    Blush fair in the glowing morn.
Over wood and tarn sweeps the glorious dawn
    To herald the Child-Christ born.

White the sea-waves fling like an angel's wing
    The foam as their blue crests rise,
While each gallant ship, with a skim and a dip,
    In the wind's lap speeding flies;
And the sailor's song is borne along
    The breeze of the golden morn,
For joyous he sings as the mast he swings
    To herald the Child-Christ born.

In the land of snow where the keen winds blow
    And the ice-king holds his sway,
A glittering sheen on the plains is seen,
    As tribute to him they pay.
While merrily sing with a peal and a ring
    The bells on the crystal morn,
As gayly they chime with silvery rhyme
    To herald the Child-Christ born.

To his sea-girt home, where'er he may roam,
  Speed the thoughts of Briton's son.
In city or plain, on the crested main,
  The heart of the absent one
Again in his dreams with ecstasy seems
  To swell in the happy morn,
As he hears the voice of his loved rejoice,
  To herald the Child-Christ born.

In dreams borne along, he joins the glad throng,
  The riot and wassail gay;
And the boar's head bold as in Nowel old
  Brave crowns the feast of the day;
The holly's red blush 'mid the ivy's crush;
  The mistletoe greets the morn
With kisses to claim in love's holy name,
  To herald the Child-Christ born.

Then Charity sweet with most gracious feet
  Walks forth o'er the smiling land,
To widow's relief, to fatherless grief,
  She bringeth a helping hand.
For peace and good-will the whole world doth fill
  With the dawn of the Nowel morn.
Let every heart sing a glad welcoming,
  To herald the Child-Christ born

Christmas Hath a Darkness

CHRISTINA ROSSETTI

Christmas hath a darkness
    Brighter than the blazing noon,
Christmas hath a chillness
    Warmer than the heat of June,
Christmas hath a beauty
    Lovelier than the world can show:
For Christmas bringeth Jesus,
    Brought for us so low.

Earth, strike up your music,
    Birds that sing and bells that ring;
Heaven hath answering music
    For all Angels soon to sing:
Earth, put on your whitest
    Bridal robe of spotless snow:
For Christmas bringeth Jesus,
    Brought for us so low.

Minstrels

WILLIAM WORDSWORTH

The minstrels played their Christmas tune
To-night beneath my cottage-eaves;
While, smitten by a lofty moon,
The encircling laurels, thick with leaves,
Gave back a rich and dazzling sheen,
That overpowered their natural green.

Through hill and valley every breeze
Had sunk to rest with folded wings:
Keen was the air, but could not freeze,
Nor check, the music of the strings;
So stout and hardy were the band
That scraped the chords with strenuous hand.

And who but listened?—till was paid
Respect to every inmate's claim,
The greeting given, the music played
In honour of each household name,
Duly pronounced with lusty call,
And 'Merry Christmas' wished to all.

Carol

KENNETH GRAHAM

Villagers all, this frosty tide,
Let your doors swing open wide,
Though wind may follow, and snow beside,
Yet draw us in by your fire to bide;
    Joy shall be yours in the morning!

Here we stand in the cold and the sleet,
Blowing fingers and stamping feet,
Come from far away you to greet—
You by the fire and we in the street—
    Bidding you joy in the morning!

For ere one half of the night was gone,
Sudden a star has led us on,
Raining bliss and benison—
Bliss to-morrow and more anon,
    Joy for every morning!

Goodman Joseph toiled through the snow—
Saw the star o'er a stable low;
Mary she might not further go—
Welcome thatch, and litter below!
    Joy was hers in the morning!

And then they heard the angels tell
"Who were the first to cry NOWELL?
Animals all, as it befell,
In the stable where they did dwell!
    Joy shall be theirs in the morning!"

Carol of the Birds

BAS-QUERCY[1]

Whence comes this rush of wings afar,
Following straight the Noël star?
Birds from the woods in wondrous flight,
Bethlehem seek this Holy Night.

"Tell us, ye birds, why come ye here,
Into this stable, poor and drear?"
"Hast'ning we seek the new-born King,
And all our sweetest music bring."

Hark how the green-finch bears his part,
Philomel, too, with tender heart,
Chants from her leafy dark retreat
Re, mi, fa, sol, in accents sweet.

Angels and shepherds, birds of the sky,
Come where the Son of God doth lie;
Christ on the earth with man doth dwell.
Join in the shout, Noël, Noël!

---

1. *Bas-Quercy* is a province in Southwestern France.

Christmas

JOHN BETJEMAN

The bells of waiting Advent ring,
    The Tortoise stove is lit again
And lamp-oil light across the night
    Has caught the streaks of winter rain
In many a stained-glass window sheen
From Crimson Lake to Hookers Green.

The holly in the windy hedge
    And round the Manor House the yew
Will soon be stripped to deck the ledge,
    The altar, font and arch and pew,
So that the villagers can say
"The church looks nice" on Christmas Day.

Provincial Public Houses blaze,
    And corporation tramcars clang,
On lighted tenements I gaze,
    Where paper decorations hang,
And bunting in the red Town Hall
Says "Merry Christmas to you all."

And London shops on Christmas Eve
    Are strung with silver bells and flowers
As hurrying clerks the City leave
    To pigeon-haunted classic towers,
And marbled clouds go scudding by
The many-steepled London sky.

And girls in slacks remember Dad,
And oafish louts remember Mum,
And sleepless children's hearts are glad.
And Christmas-morning bells say "Come!"
Even to shining ones who dwell
Safe in the Dorchester Hotel.

And is it true? And is it true,
This most tremendous tale of all,
Seen in a stained-glass window's hue,
A Baby in an ox's stall?
The Maker of the stars and sea
Become a Child on earth for me?

And is it true? For if it is,
No loving fingers tying strings
Around those tissued fripperies,
The sweet and silly Christmas things,
Bath salts and inexpensive scent
And hideous tie so kindly meant,

No love that in a family dwells,
No caroling in frosty air,
Nor all the steeple-shaking bells
Can with this single Truth compare—
That God was man in Palestine
And lives today in Bread and Wine.

Christmas, 1903

JOHN MASEFIELD

O, the sea breeze will be steady, and the tall ship 's going trim,
And the dark blue skies are paling, and the white stars burning dim;
The long night watch is over, and the long sea-roving done,
And yonder light is the Start Point light, and yonder comes the sun.

O, we have been with the Spaniards, and far and long on the sea;
But there are the twisted chimneys, and the gnarled old inns on the quay.
The wind blows keen as the day breaks, the roofs are white with the rime,
And the church-bells ring as the sun comes up to call men in to Prime.

The church-bells rock and jangle, and there is peace on the earth.
Peace and good will and plenty and Christmas games and mirth.
O, the gold glints bright on the wind-vane as it shifts above the squire's house,
And the water of the bar of Salcombe is muttering about the bows.

O, the salt sea tide of Salcombe, it wrinkles into wisps of foam,
And the church-bells ring in Salcombe to ring poor sailors home.
The belfry rocks as the bells ring, the chimes are merry as a song,
They ring home wandering sailors who have been homeless long.

A Ringer of Bells

Ted Kooser

It was like watching one of those flowing
Enlightenment dances in which each dancer
is passed hand to hand through a braiding
of partners, but this old man's partners were

the handles of bells, gloved in the soft light
of candles, silver bells placed in an order
by size, left to right, small to big, on a white
fabric-draped table set in front of the altar,

as, to a rhythm, he danced bell to bell,
his shock of white hair tossing, at first toward
the treble clef, then to the bass, eyes closed,
as he rang out those simple, sweet old carols

as if shaking the last drops of grape juice
from the cups we'd all sipped from, cups
he'd rung clean and was placing top-down
to dry, each by each, on the snowy soft cloth.

The Mystic's Christmas

John Greenleaf Whittier

"All hail!" the bells of Christmas rang,
"All hail!" the monks at Christmas sang,
The merry monks who kept with cheer
The gladdest day of all their year.

But still apart, unmoved thereat,
A pious elder brother sat
Silent, in his accustomed place,
With God's sweet peace upon his face.

"Why sitt'st thou thus?" his brethren cried,
"It is the blessed Christmas-tide;
The Christmas lights are all aglow,
The sacred lilies bud and blow.

"Above our heads the joy-bells ring,
Without the happy children sing,
And all God's creatures hail the morn
On which the holy Christ was born.

"Rejoice with us; no more rebuke
Our gladness with thy quiet look."
The gray monk answered, "Keep, I pray,
Even as ye list, the Lord's birthday.

"Let heathen Yule fires flicker red
Where thronged refectory feasts are spread;
With mystery-play and masque and mime
And wait-songs speed the holy time!

"The blindest faith may haply save;
The Lord accepts the things we have;
And reverence, howsoe'er it strays,
May find at last the shining ways.

"They needs must grope who cannot see,
The blade before the ear must be;
As ye are feeling I have felt,
And where ye dwell I too have dwelt.

"But now, beyond the things of sense,
Beyond occasions and events,
I know, through God's exceeding grace,
Release from form and time and space.

"I listen, from no mortal tongue,
To hear the song the angels sung;
And wait within myself to know
The Christmas lilies bud and blow.

"The outward symbols disappear
From him whose inward sight is clear;
And small must be the choice of days
To him who fills them all with praise!

"Keep while you need it, brothers mine,
With honest seal your Christmas sign,
But judge not him who every morn
Feels in his heart the Lord Christ born!"

Sing My Song Backwards

Brian Wren

Sing my song backwards, from end to beginning,
  Friday to Monday, from dying to birth.
Nothing is altered, but hope changes everything:
  sing "Resurrection!" and "Peace upon Earth!"

Whisper a hope through the fear of Gethsemane,
  horror and emptiness darker than night;
visit the wounds, and the failure of Calvary;
  sing "Resurrection!" and bathe them in light.

Gather the bones and the sinews of memory—
  healings and parables, laughter and strife,
joy with the outcasts and love for the enemy—
  breathe "Resurrection!" and dance them to life.

Stretch out a rainbow from cross to nativity.
  Deck out a stable with shepherds and kings,
angels and miracles, glory and poetry—
  Sing my song backwards, till all the world sings!

VI

Behold, Christmas Day Is Come
*Poems for Beholding and Remembering
Nothing Now is Common Anymore*

Now the birth of Jesus Christ was on this wise:
When as his mother Mary was espoused to Joseph,
    before they came together,
    she was found with child of the Holy Ghost.
Then Joseph her husband,
    being a just man,
    and not willing to make her a public example,
    was minded to put her away privily.
But while he thought on these things,
behold,
    the angel of the Lord
    appeared unto him in a dream, saying,
        Joseph, thou son of David,
        fear not to take unto thee Mary thy wife:
        for that which is conceived in her is of the Holy Ghost.
        And she shall bring forth a son,
        and thou shalt call his name Jesus,
        for he shall save his people from their sins.
Now all this was done,
    that it might be fulfilled
    which was spoken of the Lord by the prophet, saying,
        Behold,
        a virgin shall be with child, and shall bring forth a son,

and they shall call his name Emmanuel,
which being interpreted is, God with us.
Then Joseph
   being raised from sleep
   did as the angel of the Lord had bidden him.

From the Gospel According to Matthew, chapter 1[1]

Help us, O Lord, always to wait for Thee,
   to wish for Thee,
     and to watch for Thee,
that at Thy coming Thou mayest find us ready.

Ancient Collect, 440 AD

---

1. King James Version

Winter Trees

WILLIAM CARLOS WILLIAMS

All the complicated details
of the attiring and
the disattiring are completed!
A liquid moon
moves gently among
the long branches.
Thus having prepared their buds
against a sure winter
the wise trees
stand sleeping in the cold.

A Winter Twilight

Angelina Weld Grimké

A silence slipping around like death,
Yet chased by a whisper, a sigh, a breath;
One group of trees, lean, naked and cold,
Inking their cress 'gainst a sky green-gold;
One path that knows where the corn flowers were;
Lonely, apart, unyielding, one fir;
And over it softly leaning down,
One star that I loved ere the fields went brown.

Stopping by Woods on a Snowy Evening

ROBERT FROST

Whose woods these are I think I know.
His house is in the village though;
He will not see me stopping here
To watch his woods fill up with snow.

My little horse must think it queer
To stop without a farmhouse near
Between the woods and frozen lake
The darkest evening of the year.

He gives his harness bells a shake
To ask if there is some mistake.
The only other sound's the sweep
Of easy wind and downy flake.

The woods are lovely, dark and deep.
But I have promises to keep,
And miles to go before I sleep,
And miles to go before I sleep.

Christmas Trees

Robert Frost

(A Christmas Circular Letter)

The city had withdrawn into itself
And left at last the country to the country;
When between whirls of snow not come to lie
And whirls of foliage not yet laid, there drove
A stranger to our yard, who looked the city,
Yet did in country fashion in that there
He sat and waited till he drew us out
A-buttoning coats to ask him who he was.
He proved to be the city come again
To look for something it had left behind
And could not do without and keep its Christmas.
He asked if I would sell my Christmas trees;
My woods—the young fir balsams like a place
Where houses all are churches and have spires.
I hadn't thought of them as Christmas Trees.
I doubt if I was tempted for a moment
To sell them off their feet to go in cars
And leave the slope behind the house all bare,
Where the sun shines now no warmer than the moon.
I'd hate to have them know it if I was.
Yet more I'd hate to hold my trees except
As others hold theirs or refuse for them,
Beyond the time of profitable growth,
The trial by market everything must come to.
I dallied so much with the thought of selling.
Then whether from mistaken courtesy
And fear of seeming short of speech, or whether

From hope of hearing good of what was mine, I said,
"There aren't enough to be worth while."
"I could soon tell how many they would cut,
You let me look them over."

       "You could look.
But don't expect I'm going to let you have them."
Pasture they spring in, some in clumps too close
That lop each other of boughs, but not a few
Quite solitary and having equal boughs
All round and round. The latter he nodded "Yes" to,
Or paused to say beneath some lovelier one,
With a buyer's moderation, "That would do."
I thought so too, but wasn't there to say so.
We climbed the pasture on the south, crossed over,
And came down on the north. He said, "A thousand."

"A thousand Christmas trees!—at what apiece?"

He felt some need of softening that to me:
"A thousand trees would come to thirty dollars."

Then I was certain I had never meant
To let him have them. Never show surprise!
But thirty dollars seemed so small beside
The extent of pasture I should strip, three cents
(For that was all they figured out apiece),
Three cents so small beside the dollar friends
I should be writing to within the hour
Would pay in cities for good trees like those,
Regular vestry-trees whole Sunday Schools
Could hang enough on to pick off enough.
A thousand Christmas trees I didn't know I had!
Worth three cents more to give away than sell,
As may be shown by a simple calculation.
Too bad I couldn't lay one in a letter.
I can't help wishing I could send you one,
In wishing you herewith a Merry Christmas.

Noel

ANNE PORTER

When snow is shaken
From the balsam trees
And they're cut down
And brought into our houses

When clustered sparks
Of many-colored fire
Appear at night
In ordinary windows

We hear and sing
The customary carols

They bring us ragged miracles
And hay and candles
And flowering weeds of poetry
That are loved all the more
Because they are so common

But there are carols
That carry phrases
Of the haunting music
Of the other world
A music wild and dangerous
As a prophet's message

Or the fresh truth of children
Who though they come to us
From our own bodies
Are altogether new
With their small limbs
And birdlike voices

They look at us
With their clear eyes
And ask the piercing questions
God alone can answer.

The Tree

U. A. FANTHORPE

In the wood I am one of many.
I am felled, sold, chosen
To be sole tree of a house.
I am throned in a gold bucket.
Light is sewn through my branches,
Precious gifts wrapped in silver
Depend on my twigs. Star-crowned,
I am adored by children, cordially hated
By hoovering housewives, distrusted
By Health and Safety Officers, who name me
Fire Hazard. I reign for twelve days,
Then am sacrificed among rubbish,
Where I wither, age, decay.

But every year I rise again indoors,
Hazardous fire of love.

little tree

E. E. CUMMINGS

little tree
little silent Christmas tree
you are so little
you are more like a flower

who found you in the green forest
and were you very sorry to come away?
see   i will comfort you
because you smell so sweetly

i will kiss your cool bark
and hug you safe and tight
just as your mother would,
only don't be afraid

look   the spangles
that sleep all the year in a dark box
dreaming of being taken out and allowed to shine,
the balls the chains red and gold the fluffy threads,

put up your little arms
and i'll give them all to you to hold.
every finger shall have its ring
and there won't be a single place dark or unhappy

then when you're quite dressed
you'll stand in the window for everyone to see
and how they'll stare!
oh but you'll be very proud

and my little sister and i will take hands
and looking up at our beautiful tree
we'll dance and sing
"Noel Noel"

Christmas Lights

MICHAEL STALCUP

Everywhere we look we see
    Bright rows of stars on Christmas Eve;
    The darkness cannot but receive
Their light—even mistakenly
    Illuminating, to its fright,
    Their marvelous display at night;

And in our homes, an irony,
    The Christmas symbol ever seen:
    The never-Fall, the evergreen,
The never-dying dies so we
    Can celebrate, amidst our strife,
    The glory of a given life;

And underneath the Christmas tree,
    The gifts that everybody sees
    And wants to open early ("Please!")
Are purchased costly, given free;
    Though so long in their boxes trapped,
    One morning they will be unwrapped!

We see all this and yet forget
    The Light who shone into our depths,
    The Ever-Life who died our death,
    The Giver of immortal breath,
The God who chose to pay our debt
Before there was a Christmas yet.

Star of Wonder, Star of Light

BARBARA CROOKER

It's Christmas, the year before the accident, when the earth
still seemed fixed. My husband and children are hanging
lights on the big pine tree, the one that Becky
brought home as a seedling in first grade wrapped in a damp
paper towel. I am cooking dinner while they struggle
with the wires that somehow knot themselves up in the box.
Shadows gather behind the hills. The tree turns dark green,
then black. The tangled string unravels, and they pass it
around, loop over loop, while I watch from the steamy window:
husband, son, and daughter in a circle around the tree,
their arms full of stars.

Tinsel, Frankincense, and Fir

Dana Gioia

Hanging old ornaments on a fresh cut tree,
I take each red glass bulb and tinfoil seraph
And blow away the dust. Anyone else
Would throw them out. They are so scratched and shabby.

My mother had so little joy to share
She kept it in a box to hide away.
But on the darkest winter night—*voilà*—
She opened it resplendently to shine.

How carefully she hung each thread of tinsel,
Or touched each dime-store bauble with delight.
Blessed by the frankincense of fragrant fir,
Nothing was too little to be loved.

Why do the dead insist on bringing gifts
We can't reciprocate? We wrap her hopes
Around the tree crowned with a fragile star.
No holiday is holy without ghosts.

The Meeting

HENRY WADSWORTH LONGFELLOW

After so long an absence
    At last we meet again:
Does the meeting give us pleasure,
    Or does it give us pain?

The tree of life has been shaken,
    And but few of us linger now,
Like the Prophet's two or three berries
    In the top of the uppermost bough.

We cordially greet each other
    In the old, familiar tone;
And we think, though we do not say it,
    How old and gray he is grown!

We speak of a Merry Christmas
    And many a Happy New Year
But each in his heart is thinking
    Of those that are not here.

We speak of friends and their fortunes,
    And of what they did and said,
Till the dead alone seem living,
    And the living alone seem dead.

And at last we hardly distinguish
    Between the ghosts and the guests;
And a mist and shadow of sadness
    Steals over our merriest jests.

The House of Hospitalities

THOMAS HARDY

Here we broached the Christmas barrel,
    Pushed up the charred log-ends;
Here we sang the Christmas carol,
    And called in friends.

Time has tired me since we met here
    When the folk now dead were young.
Since the viands were outset here
    And quaint songs sung.

And the worm has bored the viol
    That used to lead the tune,
Rust eaten out the dial
    That struck night's noon.

Now no Christmas brings in neighbors,
    And the New Year comes unlit;
Where we sang the mole now labours,
    And spiders knit.

Yet at midnight if here walking,
    When the moon sheets wall and tree,
I see forms of old time talking,
    Who smile on me.

Leaves

Lynn Domina

I have been thinking
about the difference between tradition
and cliché,
and about my father,
how each December he placed a classic red poinsettia
in my mother's hands, every year the same
gold foil wrapping the planter, the same
deep green leaves, and about how lately
I bring one home, experimenting once
with the white variant which was not white
but a sallow depleted beige.
I have been thinking about repetition's
assurance, regular
as a heartbeat, its soothing familiarity
until it stops
and a man falters,
drops, not petal
by dry petal, but fully,
suddenly, gone.

Blue Christmas

BARBARA CROOKER

the name of a relatively new Advent service for mourners

This has been a dark year, when the arm of the angel of death has grown sore
from swinging his heavy scythe, eleven sharp strokes in my circle of friends.
And now it's December, when the rest of the world glitters like sugar,
when stores drip tinsel and ribbons, and the air in the mall is thick
with carols. For those who mourn, the sky is the color of soot, and white
lights hung on pines do nothing to dispel the gloom. The year burns down
to ashes, calendar pages go up in flakes of char, the reverse of birds. Going
to the store for milk and eggs before it snows is a minefield; you are bound
to bump into someone you haven't seen in years who asks about your family—
Then there's the checkout girl with the reindeer hat who brightly tells you
to have a happy holiday, and you can't reply. Sympathy cards are stuffed
in the mailbox's craw. If you can get dressed before night falls down
like a jail door clanging, it's been a good day. In the houses of mourning,
the holidays weigh like a heavy sack. In the corner, the empty chair.

Wreaths

CAROLYN HILLMAN

Red wreaths
Hang in my neighbor's window,
Green wreaths in my own.
On this day I lost my husband.
On this day you lost your boy.
On this day
Christ was born.
Red wreaths,
Green wreaths
Hang in our windows,
Red for a bleeding heart,
Green for grave grass.
Mary, mother of Jesus,
Look down and comfort us.
You too knew passion;
You too knew pain.
Comfort us,
Who are not brides of God,
Nor bore God.
On Christmas day
Hang wreaths,
Green for spent passion,
Red for new pain.

The Christmas Wreath

ANNA DE BRÉMONT

Oh! Christmas wreath upon the wall,
    Within thine ivied space
I see the years beyond recall,
    Amid thy leaves I trace
The shadows of a happy past,
    When all the world was bright,
And love its magic splendour cast
    O'er morn and noon and night.

Oh! Christmas wreath upon the wall,
    'Neath memory's tender spell
A wondrous charm doth o'er thee fall,
    And round thy beauty dwell.
Thine ivy hath the satiny sheen
    Of tresses I've caressed,
Thy holly's crimson gleam I've seen
    On lips I oft have pressed.

Oh! Christmas wreath upon the wall,
    A mist steals o'er my sight.
Dear hallow'd wreath, these tears are all
    The pledge I now can plight
To those loved ones whose spirit eyes
    Shine down the flight of time;
Around God's throne their voices rise
    To swell the Christmas Chime!

For the Birth of Christ

DANA GIOIA

Now is the season of our long regret
When all the borrowed levities conspire
To hide the hopeless balance of our debt.

The winter air grows sharp with our desire,
And all the ancient hungers reappear.
We come to watch for you, a child of fire.

Again the shining city seems so near.
Send down the flaming stairs into the night
Before our dreams have vanished with the year.

If lesser visions charmed a summer's night,
We knew they lacked the necessary pain.
You bring no season of rehearsed delight.

And requiems combine with our refrain.
For with your birth a part of us will die.
Alone, we cry the coming of your reign.

Will you, O fiery child, make no reply?

Lack of Faith

Anna Kamienska

Yes
even when I don't believe
there is a place in me
inaccessible to unbelief
a patch of wild grace
a stubborn preserve
impenetrable
pain untouched by the sleeping body
music that builds its nest in silence.

Into the Darkest Hour

MADELEINE L'ENGLE

It was a time like this,
War & tumult of war,
a horror in the air.
Hungry yawned the abyss—
and yet there came the star
and the child most wonderfully there.

It was time like this
of fear & lust for power,
license & greed and blight—
and yet the Prince of bliss
came into the darkest hour
in quiet & silent light.

And in a time like this
how celebrate his birth
when all things fall apart?
Ah! wonderful it is
with no room on the earth
the stable is our heart.

A Christmas Carol

Samuel Taylor Coleridge

I.

    The Shepherds went their hasty way,
        And found the lowly stable-shed
    Where the Virgin-Mother lay:
        And now they checked their eager tread,
For to the Babe, that at her bosom clung,
A Mother's song the Virgin-Mother sung.

II.

    They told her how a glorious light,
        Streaming from a heavenly throng,
    Around them shone, suspending night!
        While sweeter than a Mother's song,
Blest Angels heralded the Saviour's birth,
Glory to God on high! and Peace on Earth.

III.

    She listened to the tale divine,
        And closer still the Babe she pressed;
    And while she cried, the Babe is mine!
        The milk rushed faster to her breast:
Joy rose within her, like a summer's morn;
Peace, Peace on Earth! the Prince of Peace is born.

IV.

    Thou Mother of the Prince of Peace,
        Poor, simple, and of low estate!
    That Strife should vanish, Battle cease,

O why should this thy soul elate?
Sweet Music's loudest note, the Poet's story,—
Did'st thou ne'er love to hear of Fame and Glory?

V.

    And is not War a youthful King,
      A stately Hero clad in Mail?
    Beneath his footsteps laurels spring;
      Him Earth's majestic monarchs hail
Their friend, their playmate! And his bold bright eye
Compels the maiden's love-confessing sigh.

VI.

    "Tell this in some more courtly scene,
      "To maids and youths in robes of state!
    "I am a woman poor and mean,
      "And therefore is my Soul elate.
"War is a ruffian, all with guilt defiled,
"That from the aged Father tears his Child!

VII.

    "A murderous fiend, by fiends adored,
      "He kills the Sire and starves the Son;
    "The Husband kills, and from her board
      "Steals all his Widow's toil had won;
"Plunders God's world of beauty; rends away
"All safety from the Night, all comfort from the Day.

VIII.

    "Then wisely is my soul elate,
      "That Strife should vanish, Battle cease:
    "I'm poor and of a low estate,
      "The Mother of the Prince of Peace.
"Joy rises in me, like a summer's morn:
"Peace, Peace on Earth, the Prince of Peace is born."

To Jesus On His Birthday

Edna St. Vincent Millay

For this your mother sweated in the cold,
For this you bled upon the bitter tree:
A yard of tinsel ribbon bought and sold;
A paper wreath; a day at home for me.
The merry bells ring out, the people kneel;
Up goes the man of God before the crowd;
With voice of honey and with eyes of steel
He drones your humble gospel to the proud.
Nobody listens. Less than the wind that blows
Are all your words to us you died to save.
O Prince of Peace! O Sharon's dewy Rose!
How mute you lie within your vaulted grave.
    The stone the angel rolled away with tears
    Is back upon your mouth these thousand years.

Christmas Bells

HENRY WADSWORTH LONGFELLOW

I heard the bells on Christmas Day
Their old, familiar carols play,
    And wild and sweet
    The words repeat
Of peace on earth, good-will to men!

And thought how, as the day had come,
The belfries of all Christendom
    Had rolled along
    The unbroken song
Of peace on earth, good-will to men!

Till ringing, singing on its way,
The world revolved from night to day,
    A voice, a chime,
    A chant sublime
Of peace on earth, good-will to men!

Then from each black, accursed mouth
The cannon thundered in the South,
    And with the sound
    The carols drowned
Of peace on earth, good-will to men!

It was as if an earthquake rent
The hearth-stones of a continent,
    And made forlorn
    The households born
Of peace on earth, good-will to men!

And in despair I bowed my head;
"There is no peace on earth," I said;
    "For hate is strong,
    And mocks the song
Of peace on earth, good-will to men!"

Then pealed the bells more loud and deep:
"God is not dead, nor doth He sleep;
    The Wrong shall fail,
    The Right prevail,
With peace on earth, good-will to men."

A Christmas Carmen

John Greenleaf Whittier

I.
Sound over all waters, reach out from all lands,
The chorus of voices, the clasping of hands;
Sing hymns that were sung by the stars of the morn,
Sing songs of the angels when Jesus was born!
With glad jubilations
Bring hope to the nations!
The dark night is ending and dawn has begun:
Rise, hope of the ages, arise like the sun,
All speech flow to music, all hearts beat as one!

II.
Sing the bridal of nations! with chorals of love
Sing out the war-vulture and sing in the dove,
Till the hearts of the peoples keep time in accord,
And the voice of the world is the voice of the Lord!
Clasp hands of the nations
In strong gratulations:
The dark night is ending and dawn has begun;
Rise, hope of the ages, arise like the sun,
All speech flow to music, all hearts beat as one!

III.
Blow, bugles of battle, the marches of peace;
East, west, north, and south let the long quarrel cease:
Sing the song of great joy that the angels began,
Sing of glory to God and of good-will to man!

Hark! joining in chorus
The heavens bend o'er us!
The dark night is ending and dawn has begun;
Rise, hope of the ages, arise like the sun,
All speech flow to music, all hearts beat as one!

Wartime Christmas

JOYCE KILMER

Led by a star, a golden star,
The youngest star, an olden star,
Here the kings and the shepherds are,
Akneeling on the ground.
What did they come to the inn to see?
God in the Highest, and this is He,
A baby asleep on His mother's knee
And with her kisses crowned.

Now is the earth a dreary place,
A troubled place, a weary place.
Peace has hidden her lovely face
And turned in tears away.
Yet the sun, through the war-cloud, sees
Babies asleep on their mother's knees.
While there are love and home—and these—
There shall be Christmas Day.

A Belgian Christmas Eve

Alfred Noyes

Thou, whose deep ways are in the sea,
  Whose footsteps are not known,
To-night a world that turned from Thee
  Is waiting—at Thy Throne.

The towering Babels that we raised
  Where scoffing sophists brawl,
The little Antichrists we praised—
  The night is on them all.

The fool hath said . . . The fool hath said . . .
  And we, who deemed him wise,
We, who believed that Thou wast dead,
  How should we seek Thine eyes?

How should we seek to Thee for power
  Who scorned Thee yesterday?
How should we kneel, in this dread hour?
  Lord, teach us how to pray!

Grant us the single heart once more
  That mocks no sacred thing,
The Sword of Truth our fathers wore
  When Thou wast Lord and King.

Let darkness unto darkness tell
  Our deep unspoken prayer,
For, while our souls in darkness dwell,
  We know that Thou art there.

Christmas Carols

CHRISTINA ROSSETTI

1.

Whoso hears a chiming for Christmas at the nighest,
Hears a sound like Angels chanting in their glee,
Hears a sound like palm-boughs waving in the highest,
Hears a sound like ripple of a crystal sea.

Sweeter than a prayer-bell for a saint in dying,
Sweeter than a death-bell for a saint at rest,
Music struck in Heaven with earth's faint replying,
"Life is good, and death is good, for Christ is Best."

2.

A holy, heavenly chime
Rings fulness in of time,
And on His Mother's breast
Our Lord God ever-Blest
Is laid a Babe at rest.

Stoop, Spirits unused to stoop,
Swoop, Angels, flying swoop,
Adoring as you gaze,
Uplifting hymns of praise,—
"Grace to the Full of Grace!"

The cave is cold and strait
To hold the angelic state.
More strait it is, more cold,
To foster and infold
Its Maker one hour old.

Thrilled through with awestruck love,
Meek Angels poised above,
To see their God look down.
"What, is there never a Crown
For Him in swaddled gown?"

"How comes He soft and weak
With such a tender cheek,
With such a soft, small hand?—
The very Hand which spann'd
Heaven when its girth was plann'd.

"How comes He with a voice
Which is but baby-noise?—
That Voice which spake with might:
'Let there be light!' and light
Sprang out before our sight.

"What need hath He of flesh
Made flawless now afresh?
What need of human heart?—
Heart that must bleed and smart,
Choosing the better part.

"But see: His gracious smile
Dismisses us a while
To serve Him in His kin.
Haste we, make haste, begin
To fetch His brethren in."

Like stars they flash and shoot,
The Shepherds they salute.
"Glory to God" they sing;
"Good news of peace we bring,
For Christ is born a King."

3.

Lo! newborn Jesus,
Soft and weak and small,
Wrapped in baby's bands
By His Mother's hands,
Lord God of all.

Lord God of Mary,
Whom His Lips caress
While He rocks to rest
On her milky breast
In helplessness.

Lord God of shepherds
Flocking through the cold,
Flocking through the dark
To the only Ark,
The only Fold.

Lord God of all things,
Be they near or far,
Be they high or low;
Lord of storm and snow,
Angel and star.

Lord God of all men,—
My Lord and my God!
Thou who lovest me,
Keep me close to Thee
By staff and rod.

Lo! newborn Jesus,
Loving great and small,
Love's free Sacrifice,
Opening Arms and Eyes
To one and all.

Christmas

CHARLES WILLIAMS

"Let us go a journey,"
Quoth my soul to my mind,
"Past the plains of darkness
Is a house to find
Where for my thirsting
I shall have my fill,
And from my torment
I shall be still."

"Let us go a journey,"
Quoth my mind to my heart,
"Past the hills of questing,
By our ghostly art,
We shall see the high worlds,
Holy and clear,
Moving in their order
Without hate or fear."

"Let us go a journey,"
Quoth my heart to my soul,
"I shall thrive never
On the world's dole.
Past the streams of cleansing
Shall a house be found
Where is peace and healing
For my aching wound."

By the streams of cleansing,
By the hills of quest,
By the plains of darkness,
They came to their rest.
As the kings of Asia,
They went to a far land;
As the early shepherds,
They found it close at hand.

When they saw Saint Joseph
By their ghostly art,
"Forget not thy clients,
Brother," quoth my heart.
When they saw Our Lady
In her place assigned,
"Forget not thy clients,
Mother," quoth my mind.

But my soul hurrying
Could not speak for tears,
When she saw her own Child,
Lost so many years.
Down she knelt, up she ran
To the Babe restored:
"O my Joy," she sighed to it,
She wept, "O my Lord!"

Moonless Darkness Stands Between

GERARD MANLEY HOPKINS

Moonless darkness stands between.
Past, the Past, no more be seen!
But the Bethlehem-star may lead me
To the sight of Him Who freed me
From the self that I have been.
Make me pure, Lord: Thou art holy;
Make me meek, Lord: Thou wert lowly;
Now beginning, and alway:
Now begin, on Christmas Day.

What Will it Take?

Wilda Morris

The plastic manger scene on the front lawn just doesn't do it!
—MARK UNBEHAGEN

The inflatable snow man, the Santa which falls
on his face when the power is turned off,

plastic candles in the window,
turned on at dusk, off at bedtime,

department store window scenes
with dozens of mechanical elves,

don't bring me to the stable.

How long will it take me
to stumble my way there?

When will I kneel in the awe
of that not-so-silent night?

When will I pause long enough
to hear an angel song?

And when they sing, "fear not,"
will I let my heart prepare him room

and know the wonders of his love?

Christmas On the Edge

MALCOLM GUITE

Christmas sets the centre on the edge;
The edge of town, out-buildings of an inn,
The fringe of empire, far from privilege
And power, on the edge and outer spin
Of turning worlds, a margin of small stars
That edge a galaxy itself light years
From some unguessed at cosmic origin.
Christmas sets the centre at the edge.
And from this day our world is re-aligned;
A tiny seed unfolding in the womb
Becomes the source from which we all unfold
And flower into being. We are healed,
The End begins, the tomb becomes a womb,
For now in him all things are re-aligned.

Christmas Is Waiting to be Born

Howard Thurman

Where refugees seek deliverance that never comes
And the heart consumes itself as if it would live,
Where children age before their time
And life wears down the edges of the mind,
Where the old man sits with mind grown cold,
While bones and sinew, blood and cell, go slowly down to death,
Where fear companions each day's life,
And Perfect Love seems long delayed.
CHRISTMAS IS WAITING TO BE BORN:
In you, in me, in all mankind.

VII

Christmas Day and Every Day All Year Long

*Poems for Beholding and Remembering
Holy Mystery Permeates All Being*

It was there from the beginning;
We have heard it;
We have seen it
   with our own eyes;
We looked upon it,
and felt it
   with our own hands;
And it is of this we tell.
Our theme is the word of life.
This life was made visible;
We have seen it
   and bear our testimony;
We here declare to you
     the eternal life which dwelt with the Father
     and was made visible to us.
What we have seen and heard
   we declare to you,
so that you and we together
   may share in a common life,
      that life which we share with the Father
     and his Son Jesus Christ.
And we write this

in order that the joy of us all
    may be complete.

From The First Letter of John, chapter 1[1]

We beseech Thee, Almighty God,
    let our souls enjoy this their desire,
    to be enkindled by Thy Spirit,
that being filled, as lamps, by the Divine gift,
    we may shine like blazing lights
    before the Presence of Thy Son Christ at His coming.

Gelasian Sacramentary, 494 AD

1. The New English Bible

The Festival of the Nativity

RICHARD DE LEDREDE

Bestow this day on us the grace
    Upon this solemn Festival to see
    The wonder of Our Lord's Nativity.

Bestow this day on us the grace
    To order so our way of life within
    That it is free from grief or stain of sin.

Bestow this day on us the grace
    To mend our ways through life's successive hours
    And gather, as a garland, goodness' flowers.

Bestow this day on us the grace
    So blithely in the joy of God to live
    That those who hurt us, we this day forgive.

Bestow this day on us the grace
    To carol for the Birthday of our King
    And, as a gift, an honest heart to bring.

Bestow, bestow this day on us
    For healing of our griefs, His Merit's Strength,
    And bear us joyful to His Throne at length.

In Tenebris

FORD MADOX FORD

All within is warm,
   Here without it's very cold,
   Now the year is grown so old
And the dead leaves swarm.

In your heart is light,
   Here without it's very dark,
   When shall I hear the lark?
When see aright?

Oh, for a moment's space!
   Draw the clinging curtains wide
   Whilst I wait and yearn outside
Let the light fall on my face.

How the Light Comes

JAN RICHARDSON

I cannot tell you
how the light comes.

What I know
is that it is more ancient
than imagining.

That it travels
across an astounding expanse
to reach us.

That it loves
searching out
what is hidden,
what is lost,
what is forgotten
or in peril
or in pain.

That it has a fondness
for the body,
for finding its way
toward flesh,
for tracing the edges
of form,
for shining forth
through the eye,
the hand,
the heart.

I cannot tell you
how the light comes,
but that it does.
That it will.
That it works its way
into the deepest dark
that enfolds you,
though it may seem
long ages in coming
or arrive in a shape
you did not foresee.

And so
may we this day
turn ourselves toward it.
May we lift our faces
to let it find us.
May we bend our bodies
to follow the arc it makes.
May we open
and open more
and open still

to the blessed light
that comes.

Nativity

Barbara Crooker

The amaryllis bulb, dumb as dirt,
inert, how can anything spring
from this clod, this stone,
the pit of some subtropical,
atypical, likely inedible fruit?
But it does: out of the dark
earth, two shoots, green
flames in December,
despite the short days,
the Long Night Moon
flooding the hard ground.
Nothing outside grows;
even small rodents
are burrowed in
the silent nights.

Then, one morning—
a single stalk,
then a bud
that swells, bells
full sail, full bellied,
the skin grows thin,
tighter, until it splits:
heralds the night
will not be endless,
that dawn will blossom,
pearly and radiant,
and two white

trumpets unfold, sing
their sweet song,
their Hallelujah chorus,
sing carols in the thin cold air,
and our mouths say O and O and O.

Christmas Day

BRENT NEWSOM

twenty-six weeks

In bed this morning, I finally felt the kick
your mother's described for weeks to my dumb smile.
With your aunt expecting, too, we constitute
unwitting, incomplete nativities
around the den: two Marys in recliners,
your uncle and I two Josephs awaiting the blessed
events. A friend who knew such things once said
the stable was likely a cave, a room hewn out
of desert rock—not unlike a tomb.

Ritual requires we pose for a photograph,
document our growth—family of nine
this year, eleven next—so we file outside
where cardinals preen in the birdbath. We stand in rows
and smile into the merry winter light.
But the shot that we all ooh and aah about
shows two expectant mothers back to back.

This is as close to your cousin as you will come.
Ava will be cremated before you are born,
leaving your aunt and uncle only a box
of ashes they don't know where to spread.
Soon your aunt will spend sleepless nights
willing herself to feel the slightest stir.
For three long months my hand will gravitate
to the hollow cave beneath your mother's sweater.

But now the day plods on with typical cheer:
the electric noise of the boys with their R.C. cars,
their video games. The adults grazing on sweets
between hands of gin. Even the cardinals festive,
flashing their scarlet feathers at the feeder.

Breathe

MICHAEL STALCUP

This Christmas Eve
My infant son
Lies wrapped in swaddling cloths
And oxygen tubes.

Vulnerable.
Our hearts have held their breath
Too many times
For love of his little life.

Tonight I marvel
That an eternal God
Would make himself
A breathing baby boy

And, vulnerable,
Sleep in our sin-sick world—
That, having died,
We might breathe again.

Birth

KATE MCILHAGGA

To wait
to endure
to be vulnerable
to accept
to be of good courage
to go on
day after day after day;
to be heavy with hope
to carry the weight of the future
to anticipate with joy
to withdraw with fear
until the pain overcomes,
the water breaks,
and the light of the world
is crowned.
Then the travail is over,
joy has overcome.

Lord of heaven and earth,
crowned with blood
at your birth,
delivered with pain,
bring new hope to birth
in your waiting world.
Bring fresh joy
to those who weep.
Be present
in all our dyings and birthings.

Nativity

LI-YOUNG LEE

In the dark, a child might ask, *What is the world?*
just to hear his sister
promise, *An unfinished wing of heaven,*
just to hear his brother say,
A house inside a house,
but most of all to hear his mother answer,
One more song, then you go to sleep.

How could anyone in that bed guess
the question finds its beginning
in the answer long growing
inside the one who asked, that restless boy,
the night's darling?

Later, a man lying awake,
he might ask it again,
just to hear the silence
charge him, *This night*
arching over your sleepless wondering,

this night, the near ground
every reaching-out-to overreaches,

just to remind himself
out of what little earth and duration,
out of what immense good-bye,

each must make a safe place of his heart,
before so strange and wild a guest
as God approaches.

Christmas Greetings from a Fairy to a Child

LEWIS CARROLL

Lady dear, if Fairies may
For a moment lay aside
Cunning tricks and elfish play,
'Tis at happy Christmas-tide.

We have heard the children say—
Gentle children, whom we love—
Long ago, on Christmas Day,
Came a message from above.

Still, as Christmas-tide comes round,
They remember it again—
Echo still the joyful sound
"Peace on earth, good-will to men!"

Yet the hearts must childlike be
Where such heavenly guests abide:
Unto children, in their glee,
All the year is Christmas-tide!

Thus, forgetting tricks and play
For a moment, Lady dear,
We would wish you, if we may,
Merry Christmas, glad New Year!

The Bird Coop in Winter

KAREN AN-HWEI LEE

The snowdrifts are not too high, and children
    shovel the coop run on Christmas Eve.
After the storm, the birds stop laying fairy eggs
            without yolk suns
in winter. The lost fairy eggs float over the snow
never to emerge in this world—
the wind blows
and the children carry one more chicken indoors
    with a frostbitten crest
to a candlelit room of caroling and pie.

Three Magi Pass My House on a Dusky December Afternoon

Lynn Domina

At least that's how they look
to me, bundled in gold
coats, one walking
his bike, the others
just walking straight down the middle
of Arch Street as if they don't know
what a sidewalk is.
Truth be told, their coats
are brown or tan more likely, but if
I invited them in, warmed
some cider while I laundered all three garments,
they might turn out gold after all.
Boys more than men,
they still think they have something
to prove. They'd choose
Captain Morgan over cider if I let them choose,
though one at least really wants
the cider because his mother and stepfather
stopped once when he asked to stop
at a cider mill on their way home
from church, and he remembers seeing
bushels of apples tumble into the press,
and he remembers how they all sat
on the same side of a picnic table eating
cinnamon donuts, how they all
licked their fingers and grinned

sheepishly. When they leave, this one,
not the youngest though he looks youngest,
calls me *Ma'am* and reaches in his pocket
to offer me a piece of beach glass
that's been shining there
this whole time.

Too Wise Men

FRANK X WALKER

My earliest inclinations
were way too secular for membership
in the House of God youth choir, at twelve.
I was bound for hell and the little league
but if Mama needed an extra angel,
wise man or an emergency Joseph
she'd flip her old Singer to the upright position
scrape together enough thread
and a yard or two of old curtains and sheets
trusting that I knew all the words
just 'cause I lived in her house
and she played the Temptation's
Christmas album around the clock
as soon as the Thanksgiving turkey
was hash.

I didn't know frankincense from mirth
still don't, but I learned to make up
my own words to Silent Night
and to stop asking how a little baby boy
born that close to Africa to such ordinary folks
could grow up to be so white.

The Meteorology of Loss

BARBARA CROOKER

Every Christmas,
as my mailbox
is snowed in
with cards,
I shovel aside
the expected,
keep looking
for the friends
who don't write;
who've moved, don't
forward their mail,
or stop
sending cards;
somehow become lost.

My husband says
to think of the cards
I do receive:
kodaks of plum-
cheeked babies,
long, long letters;
to think of the friendships
that last, skein back
through years, fit
like old sweaters.

But I still think
of the friends
that drift away
like snowflakes,
their loss
a wind-
chill factor:
the cast off stitches,
the unwound yarn . . .

Christmas Mail

TED KOOSER

Cards in each mailbox,
angel, manger, star and lamb,
as the rural carrier,
driving the snowy roads,
hears from her bundles
the plaintive bleating of sheep,
the shuffle of sandals,
the clopping of camels.
At stop after stop,
she opens the little tin door
and places deep in the shadows
the shepherds and wise men,
the donkeys lank and weary,
the cow who chews and muses.
And from her Styrofoam cup,
white as a star and perched
on the dashboard, leading her
ever into the distance,
there is a hint of hazelnut,
and then a touch of myrrh.

Christ Climbed Down

LAWRENCE FERLINGHETTI

Christ climbed down
from His bare Tree
this year
and ran away to where
there were no rootless Christmas trees
hung with candycanes and breakable stars

Christ climbed down
from His bare Tree
this year
and ran away to where
there were no gilded Christmas trees
and no tinsel Christmas trees
and no tinfoil Christmas trees
and no pink plastic Christmas trees
and no gold Christmas trees
and no black Christmas trees
and no powderblue Christmas trees
hung with electric candles
and encircled by tin electric trains
and clever cornball relatives

Christ climbed down
from His bare Tree
this year
and ran away to where
no intrepid Bible salesmen
covered the territory

in two-tone cadillacs
and where no Sears Roebuck crèches
complete with plastic babe in manger
arrived by parcel post
the babe by special delivery
and where no televised Wise Men
praised the Lord Calvert Whiskey

Christ climbed down
from His bare Tree
this year
and ran away to where
no fat handshaking stranger
in a red flannel suit
and a fake white beard
went around passing himself off
as some sort of North Pole saint
crossing the desert to Bethlehem
Pennsylvania
in a Volkswagen sled
drawn by rollicking Adirondack reindeer
with German names
and bearing sacks of Humble Gifts
from Saks Fifth Avenue
for everybody's imagined Christ child

Christ climbed down
from His bare Tree
this year
and ran away to where
no Bing Crosby carolers
groaned of a tight Christmas
and where no Radio City angels
iceskated wingless
thru a winter wonderland
into a jinglebell heaven
daily at 8:30
with Midnight Mass matinees

Christ climbed down
from His bare Tree
this year
and softly stole away into
some anonymous Mary's womb again
where in the darkest night
of everybody's anonymous soul
He awaits again
an unimaginable
and impossibly
Immaculate Reconception
the very craziest
of Second Comings

Sugar Mice

CAROLYN HILLMAN

The Cock crows clear
On Christmas morn.
"Oooo-oo-oo-oo!"
To-day a child
Lies in the manger,
Where the brown ox
Lies too.
"Oooo-oo-oo-oo!"
"Come and see him—
A beggarwoman
Bore him last night."
"Worthless brazen hussy!—
Put her out of my barn!"
Said Grandam;
"Send her to the poor house."
"Could you not keep her
One day?" I asked.
"No indeed!" she said;
"This is Christmas,
When I must serve my black pudding,
Burning in brandy,
And when thou
Shalt see thy little tree,
Sparkling with candles,
And hung with gay sugar mice."
"But grandam,
Was not the Christ-child
Born in a manger too?"

"That was a different matter,"
She said.
The cock crowed
Three times,
Loud and clear.
"Oooo-oo-oo-oo!"
"Bastard brat
In our barn!"
"Oooo-oo-oo-oo!
Different! Different! Different!
But I slipped out to see him
And take him a sugar mouse;
And all about his head
Was a golden glory!

The House of Christmas

G. K. CHESTERTON

There fared a mother driven forth
Out of an inn to roam;
In the place where she was homeless
All men are at home.
The crazy stable close at hand,
With shaking timber and shifting sand,
Grew a stronger thing to abide and stand
Than the square stones of Rome.

For men are homesick in their homes,
And strangers under the sun,
And they lay their heads in a foreign land
Whenever the day is done.
Here we have battle and blazing eye,
And chance and honor and high surprise,
But our homes are under miraculous skies
Where the yule tale was begun.

A Child in a foul stable,
Where the beasts feed and foam,
Only where He was homeless
Are you and I at home;
We have hands that fashion and heads that know,
But our hearts we lost—how long ago!
In a place no chart nor ship can show
Under the sky's dome.

This world is wild as an old wives' tale,
And strange the plain things are,
The earth is enough and the air is enough
For our wonder and our war;
But our rest is as far as the fire-drake swings
And our peace is put in impossible things
Where clashed and thundered unthinkable wings
Round an incredible star.

To an open house in the evening
Home shall men come,
To an older place than Eden
And a taller town than Rome.
To the end of the way of the wandering star,
To the things that cannot be and that are,
To the place where God was homeless
And all men are at home.

The Gate of Eternal Blessings

Wu Li

A Poem sent to Kuo

The gate of eternal blessings
    this day has opened for you;
the light of grace and felicitation
    have come to you from Heaven.
Extirpated are your former taints,
    repulsed the Devil's troops;
now you will enjoy the real bread,
    formed in the Holy Womb.
How dignified! Your name has entered
    the register of the righteous.
How glorious! Your heart
    becomes an altar for the Lord.
I know you will prove worthy
    to console the people's yearnings;
the great hall now is in need of pillars
    raised on rock.

Christmas

—a sonnet

Each child born relives the blessed day;
Just one is Savior, but each baby glows
With something holy, halo-like, that shows
Participation in a higher way.

Yes, it will be lost; some even say
Recovery from errors and from woes
Inevitable (the onset of the blows
That mean the babe is banished from his play)

Cannot be hoped for. Yet the waning rose
Comes back again next spring in richest shades,
Its seeming death holds promise of rebirth,

And would our Father grace a flower thus,
While leaving us to wallow as life fades?
Or would the way to Heaven be through earth?

A Christmas Hymn

RICHARD WATSON GILDER

Tell me what is this innumerable throng
Singing in the heavens a loud angelic song?
    These are they who come with swift and shining feet
    From round about the throne of God the Lord of Light to greet.

O, who are these that hasten beneath the starry sky,
As if with joyful tidings that through the world shall fly?
    The faithful shepherds these, who greatly were afeared
    When, as they watched their flocks by night, the heavenly host appeared.

Who are these that follow across the hills of night
A star that westward hurries along the fields of light?
    Three wise men from the East who myrrh and treasure bring
    To lay them at the feet of him their Lord and Christ and King.

What babe new-born is this that in a manger cries?
Near on her bed of pain his happy mother lies?
    O, see! the air is shaken with white and heavenly wings—
    This is the Lord of all the earth, this is the King of Kings.

Tell me, how may I join in this holy feast
With all the kneeling world, and I of all the least?
    Fear not, O faithful heart, but bring what most is meet:
    Bring love alone, true love alone, and lay it at his feet.

Christmas in the Heart

Paul Laurence Dunbar

The snow lies deep upon the ground,
And winter's brightness all around
Decks bravely out the forest sere,
With jewels of the brave old year.
The coasting crowd upon the hill
With some new spirit seems to thrill;
And all the temple bells achime.
Ring out the glee of Christmas time.

In happy homes the brown oak-bough
Vies with the red-gemmed holly now;
And here and there, like pearls, there show
The berries of the mistletoe.
A sprig upon the chandelier
Says to the maidens, "Come not here!"
Even the pauper of the earth
Some kindly gift has cheered to mirth!

Within his chamber, dim and cold,
There sits a grasping miser old.
He has no thought save one of gain,—
To grind and gather and grasp and drain.
A peal of bells, a merry shout
Assail his ear: he gazes out
Upon a world to him all gray,
And snarls, "Why, this is Christmas Day!"

No, man of ice,—for shame, for shame!
For "Christmas Day" is no mere name.
No, not for you this ringing cheer,
This festal season of the year.
And not for you the chime of bells
From holy temple rolls and swells.
In day and deed he has no part—
Who holds not Christmas in his heart!

In the Bleak Midwinter

CHRISTINA ROSSETTI

In the bleak midwinter, frosty wind made moan,
Earth stood hard as iron, water like a stone;
Snow had fallen, snow on snow, snow on snow,
In the bleak midwinter, long ago.

Our God, Heaven cannot hold Him, nor earth sustain;
Heaven and earth shall flee away when He comes to reign.
In the bleak midwinter a stable place sufficed
The Lord God Almighty, Jesus Christ.

Enough for Him, whom cherubim, worship night and day,
Breastful of milk, and a mangerful of hay;
Enough for Him, whom angels fall before,
The ox and ass and camel which adore.

Angels and archangels may have gathered there,
Cherubim and seraphim thronged the air;
But His mother only, in her maiden bliss,
Worshipped the beloved with a kiss.

What can I give Him, poor as I am?
If I were a shepherd, I would bring a lamb;
If I were a Wise Man, I would do my part;
Yet what I can I give Him: give my heart.

The Descent of the Child

SUSAN LANGSTAFF MITCHELL

Who can bring back the magic of that story,
   The singing seraphim, the kneeling kings,
The starry path by which the Child of Glory
   'Mid breathless watchers and through myriad wings
Came, with the heaven behind Him slowly waning,
   Dark with His loss, unto the brightening earth,
The young, ennobled star, that He, so deigning,
   Chose for the heavenly city of His birth?
What but the heart of youth can hold the story,
   The young child's heart, so gentle and so wild,
It can recall the magic of that Glory
   That dreamed Itself into a little child.

Christmas Song of the Old Children

GEORGE MACDONALD

Well for youth to seek the strong,
   Beautiful, and brave!
We, the old, who walk along
   Gently to the grave,
Only pay our court to thee,
Child of all Eternity!

We are old who once were young,
   And we grow more old;
Songs we are that have been sung,
   Tales that have been told;
Yellow leaves, wind-blown to thee,
Childhood of Eternity!

If we come too sudden near,
   Lo, Earth's infant cries,
For our faces wan and drear
   Have such withered eyes!
Thou, Heaven's child, turn'st not away
From the wrinkled ones who pray!

Smile upon us with thy mouth
   And thine eyes of grace;
On our cold north breathe thy south,
   Thaw the frozen face:
Childhood all from thee doth flow—
Melt to song our age's snow.

Gray-haired children come in crowds,
    Thee their Hope, to greet:
Is it swaddling clothes or shrouds
    Hampering so our feet?
Eldest child, the shadows gloom:
Take the aged children home.

We have had enough of play,
    And the wood grows drear;
Many who at break of day
    Companied us here—
They have vanished out of sight,
Gone and met the coming light!

Fair is this out-world of thine,
    But its nights are cold;
And the sun that makes it fine
    Makes us soon so old!
Long its shadows grow and dim—
Father, take us back with him!

And Can This Newborn Mystery

Brian Wren

And can this newborn mystery,
an infant learning how to feed,
defeat the grim and chilling powers
of domination, death, and sin?
The one whose tiny hands and eyes
suspend our breath and tug our heart
awakens some to joyful praise
while others whisper, "Is it true?"

For sin infects, deceives, ensnares,
and domination towers and gleams,
and death, dispatched to foreign lands,
will turn and find us, one and all.
This child, full-grown, shall shine with love
for outcast, righteous, rich and poor,
confront the powers with healing words
and then be crushed, betrayed, destroyed.

And some will feel the Spirit's power,
and some will doubt, or cling to faith,
and some will hope but never know,
and some will joyfully believe.
And so, with doubt, or hope reborn,
or anxious certainty, or peace,
we worship, trust, and rise to serve
an infant learning how to feed.

And So the Word had Breath

Alfred, Lord Tennyson

And so the Word had breath, and wrought
  With human hands the creed of creeds
  In loveliness of perfect deeds,
More strong than all poetic thoughts;

Which he may read that binds the sheaf,
  Or builds the house, or digs the grave,
  And those wild eyes that watch the wave
In roarings round the coral reef.

The Work of Christmas

HOWARD THURMAN

When the song of the angels is stilled,
When the star in the sky is gone,
When the kings and princes are home,
When the shepherds are back with their flock,
The work of Christmas begins:

To find the lost,
To heal the broken,
To feed the hungry,
To release the prisoner,
To rebuild the nations,
To bring peace among others,
To make music in the heart.

Christ Has No Body

TERESA OF AVILA

Christ has no body but yours,
No hands, no feet on earth but yours.
Yours are the eyes with which he looks
Compassion on the world,
Yours are the feet with which he walks to do good,
Yours are the hands with which he blesses all the world.
Yours are the hands, yours are the feet,
Yours are the eyes, you are his body.
Christ has no body now but yours,
No hands, no feet on earth but yours.
Yours are the eyes with which he looks
Compassion on this world.
Christ has no body now on earth but yours.

Epilogos

Healing Prayer from Revelation

Karen An-Hwei Lee

Brew this packet of lotus leaf and lemon slices
with tracery like the rose windows in a chapel,
drop a spoonful of winter berries in boiled water,
drink deeply to mitigate our thirst, this hunger.
Pray blessings for our nations, the marred heart
of this pandemic where millions perished. Labor
in the distribution of fruit every month or daily
for all twelve. If we must dwell in this lost world,
we must till the earth. Yet our frost-bitten berries
look so lovely on the wild hawthorn apple, iced
and leafless at the turning of the year. At dawn,
our breath steams forth in the morning hymns
of teapots this season, whistling earthly clouds,
not yet heavenly ones. *On each side of the river
stood the tree of life, bearing twelve crops of fruit,
yielding its fruit every month.* With hallelujahs
and hosannas, we cherish this vision of healing,
winding our history back to the birth of Christ,
the leafy gladness of scripture as its gospel pages
set the clock ticking forward again to crucifixion
and resurrection, the goodness of an eternal gift
fleshed tenderly as figs, ruddy as pomegranates,
slender as young olives, joyful longsuffering
sown back into the soil, this present season.

Benedictus

From Light to Light

RAMI SHAPIRO

As I am enveloped in God's light,
so may I be a beacon of light
to those in search of light.
As I take shelter in God's peace,
so may I offer the shelter of peace
to those in search of peace.
As I am embraced by the Presence,
so may I be present to others
with love, justice and compassion.

Blessed are You, Lord of Light,
Who shows me Your Way
and accompanies me on my journey.
May I live the day's unfolding
with compassion and foster faith
in the One who is All.

"I will honour Christmas in my heart and try to keep it all the year."

—EBENEZER SCROOGE

A Christmas Carol, Charles Dickens

For Further Reading and Reflection

Christmas Poems

Maya Angelou, "Amazing Peace: A Christmas Poem."

Joseph Brodsky, "Star of the Nativity," "Presepio," and "25.Xii.1993" from *Nativity Poems*. New York: Farrar, Straus, and Giroux, 2001. Free download at https://archive.org/details/nativitypoemsoobrod. (U. S. Poet Laureate 1991–92).

T. S. Eliot, "Journey of the Magi" and "A Song for Simeon."

U. A. Fanthorpe. *Christmas Poems*. London: Enitharmon, 2002. https://enitharmon.co.uk/product/christmas-poems-fanthorpe

Langston Hughes, "Carol of the Brown King."

Denise Levertov, "Annunciation."

C. S. Lewis, "The Turn of the Tide" and "The Nativity."

John Milton, "On the Morning of Christ's Nativity."

Edwin Muir, "The Annunciation."

Christopher Pilling, "The Meeting Place."

Carl Sandburg, "Special Starlight."

Robert Southwell, "The Burning Babe," "New Heaven, New War," and "New Prince, New Pomp."

Henry Vaughan, "Christ's Nativity."

Books/Essays

Robert Atwan and Lawrence Wieder. *Chapters into Verse: Poetry in English Inspired by the Bible, Vol. 2.* New York: Oxford University, 1993.

Robert Atwan, George Dardess, Peggy Rosenthal. *Divine Inspiration: The Life of Jesus in World Poetry.* New York: Oxford University, 1998.

Dana Gioia. "Poetry as Enchantment." *The Dark Horse: Scotland's Transatlantic Poetry Magazine* (Summer 2015). Online: https://danagioia. com/essays/american-poetry/poetry-as-enchantment.

Jane Hirschfield. *Ten Windows: How Great Poems Transform the World.* New York: Alfred A. Knopf, 2015.

Pegram Johnson III and Edna M. Troiano, editors. *The Roads from Bethlehem: Christmas Literature from Writers Ancient and Modern.* Westminster/John Knox Press, 1993.

Mary Oliver. *A Poetry Handbook.* New York: Harcourt Brace & Company, 1994.

Mary Oliver. *Rules for the Dance: A Handbook for Writing and Reading Metrical Verse.* Boston: Houghton Mifflin, 1998.

Tania Runyan. *How to Read a Poem.* Ossining, NY: T. S. Poetry, 2014.

John Shea. *Seeing Haloes: Christmas Poems to Open the Heart.* Collegeville, MN: Liturgical, 2017.

John Shea. *Starlight.* New York: Crossroad, 1992.

WinterSong: Christmas Readings by Madeleine L'Engle and Luci Shaw. Vancouver: Regent College Publishing, 1996.

Personal Appreciations

I WISH TO EXPRESS my boundless gratitude to my Beloved, Holly Johnson, for her creative mind, her ceaseless support in this venture, and her steadfast love throughout our life journey together.

Many thanks to my faithful friends Heather Entrekin, Peter Stover, and Jim Abernathy, whose writer's eye and editing skill helped make this labor of love much better in the end than when it began.

My heartfelt gratefulness to my new friend Bonnie Thurston for gracing this work with personal reflections on poetry, Christmas, and the Incarnation. As a poet and biblical scholar, her words truly enrich all the words that follow her Foreword.

Jill Peláez Baumgaertner has been a serendipitous source of affirmation and advice.

My appreciation to Matt Wimer and the folks at Wipf & Stock for their expertise as publishers and their bold commitment to merit over market in deciding what books to publish.

Along the way on this adventure, I have crossed paths with poets who early on not only offered permission to include their poems, but also provided encouragement and affirmation of the project. My earliest communications were with Tania Runyan, Dana Gioia, Barbara Crooker, Scott Cairns, and Ted Kooser who, when I contacted him about what I was putting together and requested permission for his poem "Christmas Mail," replied that he would be delighted to be part of the book and gave me two more poems, one of which was only two days old! Then he added, "The country may be in a terrible mess but good things do happen, and your message was one of those things." Each of you with your grace and kindness has been to me one of those good things that do happen. Bless you.

And all blessings to all the poets, past and present, whose creative spirits are reflected in their words and works assembled in this anthology. Thank you for your little incarnations that help us live in another world that is this world.

The Poets

*"There is such a thing as creative solitude—a certain kind of loneliness
out of which have risen the works of the creative spirits of the past.
They were not afraid of being alone;
they had learned how to use their loneliness."*

—CARL SANDBURG

Berry, Wendell: American poet, novelist, essayist, social critic, and Kentucky farmer. Author of over 80 books of poetry, fiction, and essay. From 1979 to the present, he has been writing "Sabbath poems," one of which is, "Remembering that it happened once." *"The arts help us to converse with Paradise. Imagination permits us to see the immanence of the spirit and breath of God in the creation."*

Betjeman, John (1906–1984): English poet, writer, and United Kingdom Poet Laureate,1972–1984. On Christmas Day 1947, he wrote in a letter: *"Also my view of the world is that man is born to fulfill the purposes of his Creator, i.e., to praise his Creator, to stand in awe of Him, and to dread Him."* "Christmas" is from his *Collected Poems*.

Blake, William (1757–1827): English poet, painter, and visionary. He was a committed Christian who rejected religiosity and was hostile to the Church of England. His spiritual beliefs are reflected in *Songs of Experience* (1794) and *Songs of Innocence* (1789), which includes, "The Divine Image."

Bridges, Robert (1844–1930): British poet, United Kingdom Poet Laureate, 1913–1930, and friend and literary executor of Gerard Manley Hopkins. He studied medicine and practiced as a physician until 1881, when he devoted himself to a literary career as his full-time occupation. His poems reflect a deep Christian faith, and several of his hymns and translations continue today to be sung in worship. "Noel: Christmas Eve 1913" appeared in the *London Times*, December 24, 1913.

Brontë, Anne (1818–1848): British novelist and poet. The youngest of the three Brontë sisters, she died at age 29. "Music on Christmas Morning," is from the collection of poems by the three sisters, published under pen names that used their initials but masked their gender: *Poems by Currer, Ellis, and Acton Bell* (1846).

Cairns, Scott: American poet, memoirist, librettist, essayist who became an Orthodox Christian in 1998. He is Emeritus Professor of English at the University of Missouri and is the author of 9 poetry collections. *A School of Embodied Poetics* is the most recent. "Annunciation" and "Nativity." *"When tempted to modify your poem so that it more nearly coincides with doctrinal matter, you have to ask yourself if you are serving God or serving doctrine— are you a pilgrim or a propogandist?"*

Carroll, Lewis (1832–1898): English writer of children's fiction, mentored by his friend George MacDonald. "Christmas Greetings from a Fairy to a Child" is from *Alice's Adventures in Wonderland* (1867).

Chaves, Jonathan: Professor of Chinese at the George Washington University, Washington, D.C., award winning translator, and poet. "Christmas."

Chesterton, G. K. (1974–1936): English writer, journalist, novelist, lay theologian, Christian apologist, literary and art critic, and poet. "The House of Christmas" (1911) is from *Poems* published in 1916. *"Christmas is built upon a beautiful and intentional paradox: that the birth of the homeless should be celebrated in every home."*

Coleridge, Mary Elizabeth (1861–1907): British novelist and poet. The great grandniece of Samuel Taylor Coleridge. "I Saw a Stable" is from *Poems* (1907).

Coleridge, Samuel Taylor (1772–1834): English philosopher, theologian, poet, literary critic, and founder of English Romantic poetry with William Wordsworth. "A Christmas Carol" (1799). *"Poetry has been to me its own exceeding great reward; it has given me the habit of wishing to discover the good and beautiful in all that meets and surrounds me."*

Cranston, Pamela: Episcopal priest, author and poet who has served San Francisco Bay area congregations and hospices since her ordination in 1990.

Her books include *The Madonna Murders* (2003) and *Coming to Treeline: Adirondack Poems* (2005). "ADVENT (On a Theme by Dietrick Bonhoeffer)" is from *Searching for Nova Albion* (2019), which was a semi-finalist winner in the Poetry Society of Virginia 2020 North American Poetry Contest.

Crashaw, Richard (1613–1649) English poet, teacher, and Anglican cleric who converted to Catholicism. He is among the major metaphysical poets of 17th century English literature. "Welcome All Wonders in One Sight" is a portion of "In the Holy Nativity of Our Lord God" (1646).

Crooker, Barbara: American poet and author of nine collections of poetry. She has received multiple awards, fellowships, and residencies, and has been an invited reader at many venues, including the Library of Congress. Over 700 of her poems have appeared in numerous publications. "Nativity" (from *Small Rain*), "Star of Wonder, Star of Light" (from *Radiance*), "Blue Christmas," and "The Meteorology of Loss." *"I take as my motto something Wendell Berry once said, which is to `be joyful even though you have considered all the facts."* www.barbaracrooker.com.

Cummings, E. E. (1894–1962): American poet, painter, essayist, author, and playwright. He wrote approximately 2900 poems, 15 books of poetry, 2 autobiographical novels, 4 plays, and numerous essays. He preferred not to have his name presented in lower case letters which his publisher initiated as a marketing tactic. "little trees" first appeared in *The Dial* publication (1920).

de Brébeuf, Jean (1593–1649): French Jesuit missionary among the Hurons in "New France" (Canada). He is believed to have written the text of the "Huron Carol," Canada's oldest Christmas carol. Jesse Edgar Middleton 1926 translation.

de Brémont, Anne (1864–1922): American poet, journalist, fiction-writer, memoirist. "Christmas Morn" and "The Christmas Wreath" are from her collection, *Sonnets and Love Poems* (1892).

de Góngora, Luis (1561–1627): Spanish Baroque lyric poet. He attended the University of Salamanca and later served as chaplain to the king in Madrid. He died in Cordoba. "The Nativity of Christ" was translated from the Spanish by Henry Wadsworth Longfellow and included in *Hispanic Anthology* (1920).

de la Cruz, Juana Inés (1648–1695): Mexican nun, philosopher, composer, and considered the greatest poet of colonial Spanish America. "Christmas Day, 1689."

De Ledrede, Richard: 14th century Irish Franciscan priest and Bishop. "The Festival of the Nativity."

Deland, Margaret (1857–1945): American novelist, short story writer, and poet. "The Christmas Silence" is from her 1915 collection, *The Old Garden and Other Verses*.

de Vega, Lope (1562–1635): Prolific Spanish playwright, novelist, poet, and leading figure during the Golden Age of Spanish literature. He wrote 3000 sonnets, 3 novels, 4 novellas, 9 epic and 3 didactic poems, and 1500 plays. "A Song of the Virgin Mother" (1612) was translated from the Spanish by Ezra Pounds (1885–1970) and appeared in *Exultations of Ezra Pounds* (1909).

Domina, Lynn: American poet, professor, and Head of the English Department at Northern Michigan University. She has 2 poetry collections (*Corporal Works* and *Framed in Silence*) and is editor of a collection of essays, *Poets on the Psalms*. Her poetry has appeared in many periodicals, and her scholarly work has been published in various academic journals. She recently published, *Devotions from HERstory: 31 Days with Women of Faith*. "Leaves" and "Three Magi Pass My House on a Dusky December Afternoon." www.lynndomina.com.

Donne, John (1572–1631): English poet and Dean of St. Paul's Cathedral, London. He is recognized as one of the greatest metaphysical poets. "Annunciation" and "Nativity" from *Divine Poems* (1607).

Du Bois, W. E. B. (1868–1963): Scholar, writer, editor, civil rights pioneer, social critic, cofounder of the NAACP, and poet who said, *"Poetry, you know, is infinite labor."* "Ava! Maria!" (1908).

Dunbar, Paul Laurence (1872–1906): American poet, novelist, and playwright. Born in Ohio to freed slaves from Kentucky, he was the first African-American writer to gain an international reputation. "Christmas Carol" (1913) and "Christmas in the Heart" (1922) are from *Complete Poems* (1922).

Dutt, Toru (1856–1877): Bengali translator, essayist, and poet who published in 1877, *A Sheaf Gleaned in French Fields*, a collection of over 300

French poems translated into English, including "Christmas" by Thèophile Gautier. Her novel, *Le Journal de Mademoiselle d'Avers* was the first novel written by an Indian in French. She died of consumption at the age of twenty-one.

Fanthorpe, U. A. (1929–2009): English poet and the first woman to be nominated for the post of Professor of Poetry at Oxford. From 1974 to 2002 she wrote a brief poem to send friends as Christmas cards, including "The Wicked Fairy at the Manger," "What the Donkey Saw," "I am Joseph," "Lullaby: Sanctus Deus," "The Tree," and "Not the Millennium." *The advantage of Christmas, to a poet, is that it brings a captive audience. Friends may jib at reading poems, full-length intimidating poem, but a Christmas card can slip under anyone's guard.*" Her collection *Christmas Poems* is available at https://enitharmon.co.uk/product/christmas-poems-fanthorpe.

Ferlinghetti, Lawrence (1919–2021): An American poet, novelist, playwright, and painter. He established San Francisco's City Lights Bookstore, a center of avant-garde American literature. "Christ Climbed Down" from his collection of poems, *A Coney Island of the Mind* (1958).

Fields, Leslie Leyland: American poet, teacher, and author. She is a founding faculty member of Seattle Pacific University's MFA program and author/editor of 12 books. "Let the Stable Still Astonish" and "No Country for Two Kings." www.leslieleylandfields.com.

Ford, Ford Madox (1873–1939): English novelist, critic, editor, and poet who fought in World War I from 1915 to 1917. "In Tenebris" is from his collection, *Questions at the Wall* (1893).

Frost, Robert (1874–1963): One of the most esteemed figures in American poetry, he was the author of several poetry collections, including *New Hampshire* (1923), for which he received his first of four Pulitzer Prizes (1924, 1931, 1937, 1943). He is the only poet to receive four Pulitzers and was awarded the Congressional Gold Medal in 1960. He was nominated for the Nobel Prize in Literature 31 times. "Stopping by Woods on a Snowy Evening" from *New Hampshire* (1923) and "Christmas Trees" from *Mountain Interval* (1916).

Garrison, Theodosia (1874–1944): American poet whose collections include *The Joy O' Life, The Earth City, The Dreamers* and *As the Lark Rises.* "The Shepherd Who Stayed" is from *Christmas in Poetry* (1922).

Gilder, Richard Watson (1844–1909): American poet and editor. "A Christmas Hymn" from *Poems of Richard Watson Gilder* (1908)

Gioia, Dana: Internationally acclaimed American poet, literary critic, memoirist, past California Poet Laureate, and past chairman of the National Endowment for the Arts. He has published five collections of poems, four books of essays, written four opera libretti, and collaborated with musicians in genres from classical to jazz. "Tinsel, Frankincense, and Fir" and "For the Birth of Christ." http://danagioia.com.

Grahame, Kenneth (1859–1932): Scottish born author of *The Wind in the Willows* (1908) from which the poem "Carol" is taken as sung by a caroling group of field-mice. *". . . red worsted comforters round their throats, their fore-paws thrust deep into their pockets, their feet jiggling for warmth . . . As the door opened, one of the elder ones that carried the lantern was just saying, 'Now then, one, two, three!' and forthwith their shrill little voices uprose on the air, singing one of the old-time carols that their forefathers composed in fields that were fallow and held by frost, or when snow-bound in chimney corners, and handed down to be sung in the miry street to lamp-lit windows at Yule-time."*

Grimke, Angelina Weld (1880–958): American poet, playwright, abolitionist, feminist, and prominent figure in the Harlem Renaissance. "A Winter Twilight" is from *Negro Poets and Their Poems* (1923).

Guite, Malcolm: Anglican priest, poet, academic, and singer/songwriter. Five books of his poetry have been published. He is also author of several books on faith and theology, including *Mariner: A Voyage with Samuel Taylor Coleridge.* "Christmas on the Edge." www.malcolmguite.wordpress.com.

Hardy, Thomas (1840–1928): English poet and novelist. Nine collections of his poetry were published in his lifetime, and his novels gained more popularity after his death. "The House of Hospitalities" is from his 1909 collection, *Time's Laughingstocks and other Verses.*

Herbert, George (1593–1633) Welsh born poet and Anglican priest. "Christmas" is from *The Temple*, which was a 1633 collection of all his English poems.

Herrick, Robert (1591–1674): English country parson and lyric poet. Long neglected as a "minor poet," he came to be considered one of the most noteworthy early 17th century English poets. He became an Anglican vicar in 1630 at age 39 and served a country parish for 31 years. "A Christmas Carol" (1648).

Hillman, Carolyn: Early 20th century Massachusetts poet and translator of Hindu, Chinese, Japanese and Persian verse. "Sugar Mice" and "Wreaths" were published in *Poetry,* December 1919.

Hopkins, Gerard Manley (1844–1887): English poet and priest. He is one of the greatest poets of the Victorian era. He was raised in a devote Anglican family but became a Jesuit priest. After deciding to become a priest, he burned all his poems and for many years did not write again. His friend and fellow poet Robert Bridges ("Christmas Eve 1913") eventually edited the volume *Poems* 30 years after Hopkins's death. "The Blessed Virgin compared with the Air we Breathe" (1883) and "Moonless darkness stands between" (*Poems*, 1918).

Johnson, Emily Pauline/Tekahionwake (1861–1913): Canadian poet, critic and performer who was a popular subject of academic attention in feminism, Indigeneity, and diversity. Her father was a Mohawk chief and trained as a translator for missionaries; her mother was a middle-class Englishwoman. "Christmastide" is from her collection, *Flint & Feathers* (1914).

Johnson, Fenton (1888–1958): Born and raised in Chicago. The son of one of the city's wealthiest African American families, he attended the University of Chicago, Northwestern University, and Columbia University Graduate School of Journalism. He has been considered a forerunner to the Harlem Renaissance writers and a bridge between late 19th century writers like Paul Laurence Dunbar and the jazz rhythms of Langston Hughes. "Revery" is from *Visions of the Dusk* (1915).

Johnson, Georgia Douglas (1880–1966): Born in Atlanta, she was one of the earliest African-American female playwrights and became an important figure of the Harlem Renaissance. She published four collections of poetry: *Share My* World (1962), *An Autumn Love Cycle* (1928), The *Heart of a Woman and Other Poems* (1918) and *Bronze: a Book of Verse* (1922), for which W. E. B. Du Bois wrote the Introduction. *Bronze* includes her poem "Promise." Her author's note in *Bronze*: "*This book is the child of a bitter earth-wound. I sit on the earth and sing—sing out, and of, my sorrow. Yet, fully conscious of the potent agencies that silently work in their healing ministries, I know that God's sun shall one day shine upon a perfected and unhampered people.*" https://georgiadouglasjohnson.com.

Kamieńska, Anna (1920–1986): Polish poet, essayist, literary critic, editor, and translator. During the Nazi occupation she taught in underground village schools. She published 15 collections of her poems and translated poetry from several Slavic languages, as well as sacred texts from Hebrew and Greek. Her poems reflect the struggle of the rational mind with religious faith, and, while addressing loneliness and uncertainty, she expresses an abiding sense of gratitude for human existence. "Those Who Carry" and "Lack of Faith." "*Poetry is a presentiment of the truth.*"

Kilmer, Joyce (1886–1918): American writer and poet who was known for poetry that celebrated the natural beauty of the world and his deep religious faith. He came to Christian faith after a reading of *The Hound of Heaven.* When the United States entered World War I, he enlisted in the service and was deployed to Europe. On July 30, 1918, he was engaged in the battle of Ourcq and was killed by a sniper's bullet. After his death, a tribute to him in *Poetry Magazine* (December 1918) honored him as "having a quiet way of being genuine" with "the heart to adore and the will to worship." "The Annunciation" from *Main Street and Other Poems* (1917); "Wartime Christmas" is from *Joyce Kilmer: Memoir and Poems* (1918), Robert Cortes Holiday, editor.

Kilmore Carols: These carols, sung every year in Kilmore, Country Wexford, Ireland, are found only in this area and date back 300 years.

Kooser, Ted: Acclaimed and beloved American writer of poetry, nonfiction, and children's books, and United States Poet Laureate 2004-6. He founded and hosted "American Life in Poetry" until 2021. He is Presidential Professor Emeritus at the University of Nebraska, where he taught the writing of poetry. He has authored 26 books of poetry and nonfiction and received the 2005 Pulitzer Prize in Poetry for his book, *Delights and Shadows.* "Christmas Mail," "Harness Bells," and "Ringer of Bells." www.tedkooser.net.

Lee, Karen An-Hwei: Award winning Asian American poet, novelist, and literary critic. Her poetry, fiction, essays and translations appear in over 100 publications. Her poetry collections include *The Maze of Transparencies* (2019), *Phyla of Joy* (2012), and *In Medias Res* (2004). She is Provost and Professor of English at Wheaton College, Wheaton, IL. "Healing Prayer from Revelation" and "The Bird Coop in Winter." www.karenanhweilee.com

Lee, Li-Young: Asian American poet and memoirist whose notable awards include the American Book Award, the Whiting Award, and the Lannan Literary Award. He has authored 5 poetry collections and the memoir, *The Wingéd Seed: A Remembrance.* "Nativity." *"People who read poetry have heard about the burning bush, but when you write poetry, you sit inside the burning bush."*

L'Engle, Madeilene (1918–2007): American writer and poet who is best known for her Time Quartet: *A Wrinkle in Time, A Wind at the Door, A Swiftly Tilting Planet,* and *Many Waters.* "In the Darkest Hour." www.madeleinelengle.com.

Levertov, Denise (1923–1997): British-born-American naturalized poet whose prolific writing included protest poets, love poems, and poetry reflective of her faith in God. She died of cancer at age 74, and continued composing poetry nearly to the moment of death. Forty of her last poems were published in 1999, *The Great Unknowing.* "On the Mystery of the Incarnation." *"In certain ways writing is a form of prayer."*

Longfellow, Henry Wadsworth (1807–1882): American poet and educator who was a traveler, a linguist and a romantic rooted in American life and history, while identifying with the literary traditions of Europe. "Christmas Bells" from *Flower-De-Luce* (1866), "The Meeting," from *Birds of Passage, Flight the Third* (1873) and "The Three Kings" from *Birds of Passage, Flight the Fifth* (1878). Translator of "The Nativity of Christ" by Luis de Góngora.

MacDonald, George (1824–1905): Scottish pastor, theologian, poet, novelist, writer of Christian fantasy and fairytales. He was forced out of the church he served because of his resistance to Calvinism's God-electing love of some and his affirmation of God's universal love for all. His friendships included Lewis Carroll, Alfred, Lord Tennyson, Matthew Arnold, and during his American lecture tour in 1872, he became friends with nearly every well-known writer, including Mark Twain, Walt Whitman, Oliver Wendell

Homes, and Henry Wadsworth Longfellow. Writers such as C. S. Lewis, W. H. Auden, J. M. Barrie (*Peter Pan*), Frank Baum (*Wizard of Oz*), G. K. Chesterton, and Madeleine L'Engle acknowledged his influence on them. "The Mother Mary" (*A Hidden Life and other poems*, 1864); "A Christmas Carol" (*Poems*, 1893); "Far Across the Desert Floor" (portion of "An Old Story"), "Christmas Song of the Old Children," and "A Christmas Prayer" (from *Poetical Works*, 1915).

Masefield. John (1878–1967): English poet, novelist, dramatist who was appointed British Poet Laureate in 1930 and held the office until his death in 1967. "Christmas Eve at Sea" from *Salt-Water Poems and Ballads* (1916) and "Christmas, 1903" from his *The Story of a Round-House and Other Poems* (1914).

McIlhagga, Kate (1938–2002): A member of the Iona Community on the island of Iona in Scotland for which she composed poems and prayers, including "Birth."

Millay, Edna St. Vincent (1892–1950): American lyric poet and playwright. She was one of the most successful and admired American poets of her time, and a leading voice for new kinds of female experiences and expressions in male-dominated American life and society. Her collection of poems, *The Ballad of the Harp-Weaver and other poems*, won the 1923 Pulitzer Prize. "To Jesus On His Birthday" was first published in *The Buck in the Snow and Other Poems* (1928). www.millay.org.

Mitchell, Susan Langstaff (1866–1926): Irish poet and writer, known for her quick wit and stinging satire. She was born in Carrick-on-Shannon, Co. Leitrim, and, while she was a Protestant, she rejected unionist belief and supported Home Rule with strong republican sympathies, and was a prominent voice engaged in the debates about the changing nature of gender relations. Her friends include W. B. Yeats. Her mother was Sligo memoirist Kate Cullen. "Descent of the Child," "The Child in the Manger," and "The Star of the Heart" are from her 1908 collection, *The Living Chalice and other Poems*.

Monroe, Harriet (1860–1936): American editor, scholar, literary critic, poet and founding publisher and long-time editor of *Poetry: A Magazine of Verse* first published in 1912. "How Would You Paint God?" is excerpted from her poem "Their God," which appeared in the March 1924 edition of

Poetry. "*If we cheapen the Christmas festival—if we use the great historical festival as a mere medium of exchange, if we give no thought to the inner spiritual significance which has made it a symbol of hope to uncounted millions since the birth night at Bethlehem, we thereby refuse beauty and accept sordidness, we refuse truth and accept a sham.*"

Montgomery, Helen Barrett (1861–1934): American social reformer, writer, and educator. In 1899, she was the first woman elected to the Rochester (NY) School Board, 20 years before women could vote. In 1921, she was the first woman elected president of any religious denomination in the United States (Northern Baptist Convention, today American Baptist Churches USA). In 1924, she was the first woman to publish a translation of the New Testament from the original Greek. "Mary's Magnificat" is her translation of the ancient poetic text recorded in Luke 1:47–55.

Morris, Wilda: American poet, writer, ordained minister and former seminary faculty member. She is Workshop Chair of Poets & Patrons of Chicago and a past President of the Illinois Poetry Society. Her published poems include *Pequod Poems: Gamming with Moby Dick* (Kelsay Books). "A Shepherd Boy Remembers," "The Innkeeper's Regrets," and "What Will It Take?" Wildmorrs.blogspot.com.

Nesdoly, Violet: Canadian poet, author, and artist whose special interest is "*capturing the ordinary stuff of life with pencil, pen and paints.*" "How the Natal Star Was Born." www.violetnesdoly.com.

Newsom, Brent: Oklahoma poet and professor who received the Maureen Egen Writers Exchange Award in poetry from *Poets & Writers,* and the Foley Poetry Prize from *America.* He wrote the libretto for *A Porcelain Doll,* an opera based on the life of deaf-blind pioneer Laura Bridgman, and is the author of *Love's Labors* (CavanKerry Press, 2015). His poems have also appeared in numerous journals. "Make Way" and "Christmas Day."

Noyes, Alfred (1880–1958): English poet who published his first poetry collection, *The Loom Years,* in 1902 at age 21. He published 15 poetry collections, along with short stories, essays, literary criticism, plays, and autobiography. Over time his increasing blindness required him to dictate his works in later life. "A Belgian Christmas Eve" is the Dedication in his play, *Rada,* a drama of war in one act (1915).

Porter, Anne (1911–2011): American poet who published her first collection of poems, *An Altogether Different Language*, at age 83, and was named a finalist for the National Book Award. *"People don't use their creativity as they get older. They think this is supposed to be the end of this and the end of that. But you can't always be so sure that it is the end."* She died just a month shy of her 100th birthday. "Noel."

Prudentius (348–405): Roman poet who practiced law, was twice a provincial governor, and served in the court of Roman Emperor Theodosius. He tired of court life, withdrew into solitude, and devoted the remainder of his days to being an ascetic, writing poetry on Christian themes. "Of the Father's Love Begotten" (Translation from Latin by J. M. Neale, (1851), extended by Henry W. Baker, (1861); Roby Furley Davis trans. stanzas 2, 7, 8, 9 (1906).

Richardson, Jan: American poet, artist, writer, author of 8 books, and ordained United Methodist minster. "How the Light Comes." www.janrichardson.com.

Rice, Albert (1903-?): A poet of the Harlem Renaissance. "The Black Madonna" appeared in *Palms* poetry magazine (1926), Idella Purnell, editor. Of the poem he said, *"I was one evening at vespers down at St. Mary's the Virgin, and while lost in contemplation before Our Lady, I thought of a Madonna of swart skin, a Madonna of dark mien."*

Rios, Alberto: American poet, educator, and memoirist whose poems and short stories reflect his Chicano heritage. He has published 10 books and chapbooks of poetry, and 3 collections of short stories. He was named Arizona's first poet laureate in 2013 and continues to hold that esteemed honor. "When Giving Is All We Have," about which he said: *"This is a poem of thanks to those who live lives of service, which, I think, includes all of us—from the large measure to the smallest gesture, from care-giving to volunteerism, to being an audience member or a reader. I've been able to offer these words to many groups, not only as a poem but also as a recognition. We give for so many reasons, and are bettered by it."*

Rossetti, Christine (1830–1894): English poet and author of *Goblin Market and Other Poems* (1862) and *A Pageant and Other Poems* (1881). "Christmas Hath a Darkness" (published in 1893 as "Christmas Eve"), "In the Bleak Midwinter," (1872), and "Christmas Carols" (c. 1887) from *Poetical Works of Christina Georgina Rossetti* (1904).

Rowe, Noel (1951–2007): Australian priest, poet, essayist, and academic. He was Senior Lecturer in Australian Literature at the University of Sydney. Before becoming an academic, he was a priest in the Marist Order. His special interest was the interconnectedness of literature, theology and ethics. He published 3 books of poetry with Vagabond Press: *Perhaps, After All, Next to Nothing,* and *Touching the Hem.* "Magnificat: Annunciation." *"When I am writing I am as close as I get to being fully alive, but I am only writing well if I am not thinking about myself."*

Runyan, Tania: American poet, author, and teacher. Her poetry books include *What Will Soon Take Place, Second Sky, A Thousand Vessels, Simple Weight,* and *Delicious Air.* She has written poetry field guides on *How to Write a Poem, How to Write a Form Poem,* and *How to Read a Poem.* "The Angel at the Nativity," "The Shepherd at the Nativity," "Joseph at the Nativity," and "Mary at the Nativity." www.taniarunyan.com.

Sandburg, Carl (1878–1967): American poet, biographer, journalist, and storyteller who received the Pulitzer Price twice for his poetry (*Corn Huskers,* 1919; *Collected Poems,* 1951) and once for his biography *Abraham Lincoln: The War Years* (1940). "Star Silver."

Shapiro, Rami: American rabbi, poet, and prolific author on spirituality. "From Light to Light." rabbirami.com.

Shea, John: Chicago native theologian, storyteller, author, and poet. He has written over 20 books of theology and spirituality, 3 works of fiction, and 3 books of poetry. He lectures nationally and internationally on storytelling, contemporary spirituality, and faith-based health care. "Sharon's Christmas Prayer." www.johnshea.com.

Stalcup, Michael: Thai American missionary and poet living in Bangkok, Thailand with his wife and three children. "Breathe" and "Christmas Light." He wrote "Breathe" in the hospital room beside his two-month-old son who was on oxygen for bronchiolitis (and who made it through just fine). www.michaelstalcup.com.

Stott, Roscoe Gilmore (1880–1957): Indiana born poet and writer. "Joseph and Mary" from *The Man Sings* (1914).

Teasdale, Sara (1884–1933): American poet who authored 7 books of poetry and was popular with the public and critics during her lifetime. She won the 1918 Columbia Poetry Prize, later renamed the Pulitzer Prize for Poetry. "Christmas Carol" from *Helen of Troy and Other Poems* (1911) and "In the Carpenter's Shop" from *Rivers to the Sea* (1915).

Tennyson, Alfred, Lord (1809–1892): The most renowned English poet of the Victoria era who served as Poet Laureate upon the death of William Wordsworth. "Ring Out, Wild Bells" and "And so the Word had breath," are from *In Memoriam* XXXIII and XXXVI (1850).

Teresa of Avila (1515–1582): Spanish Carmelite mystic, reformer and writer. "Christ Has No Body."

Thurman, Howard (1899–1981): American author, theologian, poet, pastor, leading voice for social justice, and mentor to many leaders of the civil rights movement, including Martin Luther King, Jr. He authored 20 books on theology, philosophy, and religion, and was co-founding pastor with white pastor Alfred Fisk of Church for the Fellowship of All Peoples in San Francisco, the first interracial and interdenominational church in America. "The Work of Christmas" and "Christmas is Waiting to be Born."

Thurston, Bonnie: American poet, theologian, author, New Testament scholar, ordained Disciples of Christ minister, and licensed lay reader in the Episcopal Church. She is an internationally recognized Thomas Merton scholar and is the author/editor of 23 theological works and 6 collections of poetry. As a native West Virginian, she lives a quiet life in Wheeling, WV. "Lucubrations" and "Silent Night." *"Poetry takes the heart's hands and transports it to places it cannot otherwise go."*

Underhill, Evelyn: (1875–1941): Anglican lay leader and theologian, author and poet. She was a prolific writer focusing on the spiritual life and mysticism, with 39 books and over 350 articles and reviews. Her poetry collections are *The Bar-Lamb's Ballad Book* (1902), *Theophanies* (1916), and *Immanence* (1916), which includes "Two Carols." www.evelynunderhill.org.

Waddinge, Luke (1600–1691): Irish poet and bishop of Ferns. "For Christmas Day" first appeared in *A Small Garland of Pious and Godly Songs*, 1684.

Walker, Frank X: Kentucky poet, University of Kentucky professor, and founding member of Affrilachian Poets. *Affrilachia: Poems, The Affrilachian Sonnets,* and *Black Box* are among his poetry collections. He edited the anthology, *America! What's My Name? The "Other" Poets Unfurl the Flag.* "Too Wise Men." *"As a writer/observer/truth teller, I choose to focus on social justice issues as well as multiple themes of family, identity, and place."* www. frankxwalker.com.

Whittier, John Greenleaf (1807–1892): American Quaker poet, journalist, writer, and a leading anti-slavery voice in his time. "A Christmas Carmen" (1873) and "The Mystic's Christmas" (1882) from *The Poetical Works of John Greenleaf Whittier,* edited by W. Garrett Horder (1911).

Widdemer, Margaret (1884–1978): American poet and novelist. She gained public attention with her 1915 poem focusing on child labor, "The Factories," and won the 1919 Pulitzer Prize (then the Columbia University Prize) for her collection, *The Old Road to Paradise.* The Prize was shared that year with Carl Sandburg for *Cornhuskers.* "A Ballad of the Wise Men" is from her Prize-winning collection.

Wilde, Oscar (1854–1900): Irish playwright (*The Importance of Being Ernest,* 1895), novelist (*The Picture of Dorian Gray* 1890), poet. He died in poverty in Paris. "Ave Maria Gratia Plena" (1881). *"The moment that an artist takes notice of what people want, and tries to supply the demand, he ceases to be an artist."*

Williams, Charles (1886–1945): British poet, playwright, theologian, literary critic, biographer, novelist, and a member of the *Inklings,* an informal literary discussion group at Oxford University. The other 2 members of the group of 3 were C. S. Lewis and J. R. R. Tolkien. Williams published nearly 40 books, and his first poetry collection was *The Silver Stair* in 1912. "Christmas" is from his 1924 collection, *Windows of Night.* www.charleswilliamssociety.org.uk.

Williams, William Carlos (1883–1963): Puerto Rican-American poet, novelist, essayist, playwright, and physician who began his medical practice in New York City's notorious neighborhood of "Hell's Kitchen" and continued to practice for 40 years in Rutherford, NJ. He is recognized as an experimenter and innovator in American poetry. "The Gift" and "Winter Trees" (1921). *"A poem is a small (or large) machine with words."*

Wordsworth, William (1770–1850): A founder of English Romantic poetry with his friend Samuel Taylor Coleridge, with whom he co-wrote *Lyrical Ballads*, for which Wordsworth is most known. He was named Poet Laureate of England in 1843. "Minstrels" is from his collection, *The River Duddon: A Series of Sonnets* (1820). *"Poetry is the spontaneous overflow of powerful feelings; it takes its origin from emotion recollected in tranquility."*

Wren, Brian: Internationally published hymn-poet whose texts appear in hymnals of all Christian traditions. He was ordained in Britain's United Reformed Church. He has authored 11 books and numerous articles focused around worship and is emeritus Professor of Worship at Columbia Theological Seminary, Decatur, GA. "Good is the Flesh," "Sing My Song Backwards," and "And Can This Newborn Mystery?"

Wu Li (1632–1718): Chines landscape painter, calligrapher, and poet who lived during the Qing Dynasty. He converted to Christianity and became a Jesuit priest in 1688. He expressed his Christian faith in poetry, making him the earliest Chinese Christian poet. "The Gate of Eternal Blessings" was translated by Jonathan Chaves.

Yeats, William Butler (1865–1939): Irish poet, dramatist, prose writer, regarded as Ireland's greatest modern poet and recipient of the Nobel Prize in 1923. He co-founded the Abbey Theatre in Dublin. He died in France and is buried in Drumcliffe Churchyard, County Sligo, Ireland. "The Magi" from *Responsibilities* (1914). *"By logic and reason we die hourly; by imagination we live."*

More extensive biographies of many of these poets are available at the website of the Poetry Foundation (www.poetryfoundation.org/poets), and at Academy of American Poets (https://poets.org).

Bibliography

Brueggemann, Walter. *Finally Comes the Poet: Daring Speech for Proclamation.* Minneapolis: Fortress, 1989. "Introduction," 1–12.

Buechner, Frederick, *Whistling in the Dark.* San Francisco: Harper & Row, 1988.

———. *Wishful Thinking: A Theological ABC.* New York: Harper & Row, 1973.

Burrows, Mark., *The Paraclete Poetry Anthology.* Brewster, MA: Paraclete, 2016.

Chesterton, G. K. *Orthodoxy.* New York: Doubleday, 1990.

Gioia, Dana. "Poetry as Enchantment." *The Dark Horse: Scotland's Transatlantic Poetry Magazine* (Summer 2015). Online: https://danagioia.com/essays/american-poetry/poetry-as-enchantment/

Goodspeed, Edgar J. *The New Testament.* Chicago: University of Chicago Press, 1923.

Heschel, Abraham. *Man Is Not Alone.* New York: Farrar, Straus & Young, 1951.

Hirshfield, Jane. *Nine Gates: Entering the Mind of Poetry,* New York: HarperCollins, 1997.

———. *Ten Windows: How Great Poems Transform the World.* New York: Alfred A. Knopf, 2015.

Johnson, Dennis L. *To Live in God: Daily Reflections with Walter Rauschenbusch.* Valley Forge, PA: Judson, 2020.

Kooser, Ted. *The Wheeling Year: A Poet's Field Book.* Lincoln, NE: University of Nebraska Press, 2014.

Koss, Erika. "A Conversation with Dana Gioia," *Image* 73. Online: https://imagejournal.org/article/conversation-dana-gioia/

Lamb, Zachary. "Life According to Seamus Heaney." National Endowment for the Arts. March 13, 2018. Online: https://www.arts.gov/stories/blog/2018/life-according-seamus-heaney.

L'Engle, Madeleine. *The Glorious Impossible.* New York: Simon & Schuster, 1990.

L'Engle, Madeleine and Luci Shaw. *WinterSong: Christmas Readings by Madeleine L'Engle and Luci Shaw.* Vancouver: Regent College, 1996.

Lewis. C. S. *Reflection on the Psalms.* London: Geoffrey Bles, 1958.

———. *The Grand Miracle.* New York: Ballantine, 1983.

MacDonald, George. "My Uncle Peter," *Adela Cathart.* London: Samson Lowe, Marston, Searle & Rivington, 1882.

———. *Without and Within.* London: Scribner, Armstrong, & Co., 1872.

Merton, Thomas. *Dialogues with Silence: Prayers and Drawing.* Edited by Jonathan Montaldo. New York: HarperCollins,2001.

Montgomery, Helen Barrett. *The Centenary Translation: The New Testament in Modern English.* Philadelphia: Judson, 1924.

Muto, Susan Annette. *Pathways to Spiritual Living.* Petersham, MA: St. Bede's, 1984.

Bibliography

Nouwen, Henri. *The Living Reminder: Serving and Prayer in Memory of Jesus.* New York: Seabury, 1977.

Oliver, Mary. *Evidence.* Boston: Beacon, 2009.

———. *A Poetry Handbook: A Prose Guide to Understanding and Writing Poetry.* New York: Harcourt Brace &Company, 1994.

Runyan, Tania. *How to Read a Poem.* Ossining, NY: T. S. Poetry, 2014.

Shea, John. *An Experience Named Spirit.* Chicago: Thomas Moore, 1983.

———. *Seeing Haloes: Christmas Poems that Open the Heart.* Collegeville, MN: Liturgical, 2017.

Thurman, Howard. *The Mood of Christmas & Other Celebrations.* Richmond, IN: Friends United, 1973.

———. *Deep Is the Hunger.* Richmond, IN: Friends United, 2000.

Tuten, Nancy Lewis and John Zubizarreta, eds. *The Robert Frost Encyclopedia.* Westport, CT: Greenwood, 2001.

Wren, Brian. "Poet of Faith: An Interview with Brian Wren." www.reformedworship.org. April 28, 2020.

Yeats, William Butler. *The Land of Heart's Desire.* Portland, ME: Thomas B. Moser, 1906.

Made in United States
North Haven, CT
03 December 2022

27769376R00163